Karezza and the Karezza Method

Karezza and the Karezza Method

The Classic Western Approach to Tantric Sexual Healing

ALICE B. STOCKHAM, M.D.

J. WILLIAM LLOYD

Karezza and the Karezza Method:
The Classic Western Approach to Tantric Sexual Healing
Alice Bunker Stockham (1833–1912)
John William Lloyd (1857–1940)
Copyright © Alice Stockham 1903
ISBN 978-1492160694

Contents

KAREZZA

Alice B. Stockham

	Preface	*9*
1	Creative Energy	12
2	Karezza	19
3	Attainment Possible	24
4	Health	28
5	Parenthood	34
6	Control of Procreative Powers	37
7	Free Motherhood	43
8	Married and Mated	48
9	Procreation of Thought	59
10	Spiritual Growth	64

THE KAREZZA METHOD
J. William Lloyd

	Preface	*91*
1	What Is Karezza?	94
2	Magnetation	107
3	Cleanness	112
4	Sex and Soul	113
5	When Sex Satisfies	115
6	Duality and Spirituality in Sex	117
7	Sex-Commerce and the Elixir of Life	122
8	The Wine of Sex	126
9	The Karezza Method	129
10	The Woman's Part in Karezza	135
11	The Woman's Time of Great Desire	140
12	Does Woman Need the Orgasm?	143
13	The Woman's Shock	146
14	Psychic Impotence	149
15	Karezza the Beautifier	158
16	The Danger of Excess	161
17	Final Considerations	165
	Appendix	*173*

KAREZZA

Preface

The author's work *Tokology* was written from years of professional experience to meet a demand among inquiring women on subjects that deeply concern the physical life of the wife and mother. In these later years, the world of thought has grown, and new discoveries have been made in spiritual as well as material science.

In answer to hundreds of letters of inquiry, I send out this message, *Karezza*, elucidating a theory of conjugal life in which there is a love-communion between husband and wife, from which results a mastery of the physical and complete control of the fecundating power.

In *The Familiar Letter of Tokology*, subjects usually considered delicate in nature and difficult to handle are presented indirectly and briefly. In an early edition, those interested in a "wiser parentage" are cited to a pamphlet written by a distinguished minister, Rev. John Humphrey Noyes, who therein had given to the world a new and unique theory of controlling propagation. Afterward, to my regret and the disappointment of numerous correspondents, it was discovered that the work was out of print.

In later editions of *Tokology*, alluding to methods of limiting offspring, the following paragraph occurs: "By some a theory called 'sedular absorption' is advanced. This involves intercourse without culmination. No discharge is allowed. People practicing this method claim the highest possible enjoyment, no loss of vitality, and perfect control of the fecundating power."

Many readers asked for further explanation. It proved that the word "sedular" is not found in the dictionaries but, as used in this connection, means pertaining to seed and is so defined in the glossary of the book.

Karezza elucidates the above paragraph; gives a high ideal to parental functions; pleads for justice to the unborn child; teaches that the control of procreation is possible with every husband and wife; gives honor to womanhood; and, most of all, controverts the prevailing ideas of baseness and degradation associated with the sexual nature.

Karezza may be considered a supplement to *Tokology* and, like that, deals with tested theories and practical truths. They have been lived and demonstrated, and are here presented as living facts.

Men and women must learn the significance of the sexual relation, and its possible influence upon life and character. Copulation is more than a propagative act; it is a blending of body, soul, and spirit, ennobling or degrading according to the attitude of the participants. For both husband and wife, it has a function in soul-development that hitherto has been prevented and perverted by the traditional uncleanness attached to the relation. Nature made but one mistake in the evolution of life, according to man's edict, and that is in creating the human reproductive organs. Reverse this edict. Let the searchlight of truth illumine this subject, and a satisfactory solution of many social problems will be evolved. No part of the body should be under condemnation. The young should be enlightened upon these important subjects, while the knowledge of sexual science will open the door for the true marriage.

Karezza makes a plea for a better birthright for the child and aims to lead individuals to seek a higher development of themselves through the most sacred relations. It presents truths that are attainable, and when the goal of mastery is reached, the ideal marriage will be consummated in united lives, giving a prophecy of generations of desired and welcome offspring.

A. B. S.

CHAPTER 1

Creative Energy

Let there be light.

Man is a trinity of spirit, soul, and body. Spirit is the source or God-life of man, from which all proceeds. Soul is Spirit in action and embraces all that is recognized as individual, personal existence. Soul includes the intellect, the emotions, and the sensations. It is the thinking, loving, living realm of man. From the Spirit, through conscious training, one is capable of developing unlimited forces and possibilities. Soul looks within to the all for life, knowledge, and power, which it expresses through the physical. As thought precedes action, so nothing can appear or manifest itself in the body that has not been conceived or thought of in the soul. Soul may recognize Spirit as a governing principle, or it may look out through the senses for material manifestations, depending only upon symbols for its concept of life.

Voluntarily and consciously man may choose between these two roads—the spiritual or material. In his philosophy, he may recognize that all power and all life are from and of the Spirit; or, he may attribute all development, all growth, all evolution to matter.

In the spiritual view, recognizing the divine principle as an ever-present, active energy, as life and intelligence operating through the soul upon matter, one comes to conclusions that make all of life's problems less difficult.

Creative energy, expressing through the sexual nature an instinct to perpetuate life, has its origin in, and is coexistent with, life itself. It is the power behind all purposes and plans. It is the self-impelling force that gives the ability to do and perform. It is the origin of all activities of child life. It is the inventive genius and impelling factor of all man's handiwork—the thought force of mechanics and machinery.

Both the macrocosms and microcosms of the universe are expressions of the law of life, instinctively put forth by creative energy. This force operates in the multiplication of atoms, in the drawing of the pollen upon the stigma, in the attraction of sperm to germ cells. It is the segregation and aggregation of all molecules of matter, founded upon the duality of sex.

The processes of growth and fulfillment of the functions are propelled by this omnipresent energy of spirit, which is inherent in, and operative through, all nature. It is behind the physical life of man and other animals, and expresses itself through them. Only when it comes with the strong voice of life demanding perpetuation is it especially a manifestation of the sex-nature—a fulfillment of the law of growth, of development, and of increase. Atoms, cells, and plants are unconscious of this life-force, and animals conscious only in a small degree.

Man not only has consciousness of this energy, but through his intelligence is capable of developing greater consciousness of its operation and the law governing it. He knows that he knows, and in this knowledge lies his superiority over the brutes.

This recognition and knowledge makes it possible for man to train this creative potency in all life's purposes and uses. From the inception of the bud of life to its fructifying stage, man may be the master and maker of his conditions. There is no karma for him that is not within his own power to mold and make; no passion to usurp authority, no desire that he may not guide and direct. The perfectness of his nature is evolved through the recognition, direction, and appropriation of the creative energy, the occult force of life.

Sexual science based upon this theory teaches that there are deeper purposes and meanings to the reproductive faculties and functions than are generally understood and taught.

In the physical union of male and female, there may be a soul communion giving not only supreme happiness, but in turn conducing to soul growth and development. There may also be a purpose and power in this communion, when rightly understood, not less significant than the begetting of children. Creative energy in man is manifold in its manifestations and can be trained into channels of usefulness. Consciously, it may be utilized in every activity, devising, inventing, constructing. It may be directed to building bodily tissue and permeating every cell with health and vigor. Sex in nature is universal, progressing from lower to higher manifestations of life; it is more distinctive as male and female.

Sexual instinct or passion is a sure sign of seed germination; it is an indication that life may be perpetuated, and that the entire man or woman is in preparation for the culmination of being. It is not an instinct or power either to be ignored or destroyed. Its perversion means physical and spiritual degeneracy.

Seed production is the goal or highest function of tree or plant, and procreation is the complete or ultimate manifestation of man's life. Reproduction is the fulfillment of divine law.

In the plant and in the tree, the life principle fulfills the law of its being in bearing seed. Its manifestation in man is procreation, reproducing another of its kind. Passion is the instinct for the preservation of one's kind, the voice and the sign of creative power. The highest mission in rose-life is to produce seeds, but on its way it gives beautiful blossoms and fragrant perfume. It may not always be able to fulfill its highest mission, but it can express creative power on its way to fulfillment to the production of seeds. Man, too, expresses creative life in many ways besides that of parenthood. He preaches a sermon, writes a book, invents a machine. Woman writes a "Battle Hymn of the Republic," or makes a loaf of nutritious bread. In both the least and the greatest things of life, man gives expression to inherent creative principle.

An artist is a creator. Emerson gives the keynote when he says, "Work your passion up into poetry." So with all things, the life principle demanding fulfillment is the power on its way to accomplishment. When the signs of this creative power come throbbing and pulsating into every fiber, it only shows that one has greater ability to create than ever before. There are varied and definite appropriations for this energy.

Knowledge of the law of the spirit gives the ability to control this power and all its signs. One becomes its master as truly as is the engineer of his engine, or the electrician of the most potent force known to man. The physical sign appearing as passion is of the spirit and not of the flesh. Treat it as the voice of a power impelling one to do, to work. Say quickly: "What new work is before me? I am a creator. What shall I create?" The sign is a proof of strength and ability to do greater things than yet accomplished. Demand of the spiritual-self to know what that work may be. Listen, listen to the voice; the intuition or Higher Self in the silence of the soul will give answer. Then think, plan, and work for fulfillment.

Religion and philosophy are required in consecrating passion. One inspires a faith in the source of all power, the other defines man's relation to that power. Already, perhaps, the heart-life is devoted to some great work, some mission to humanity. But now include directly and specifically in this consecration creative energy, the inherent, impelling, burgeoning force of life. This inherent force is so prominent in its demands, so ever-present in action, and intrinsically so allied to cosmic force, that it deserves and requires a special consecration. It must be known as good and not evil, as a friend and not an enemy, as a quickening, generating power. Consciously, thoughtfully, and specifically command its service. In no way does man's do minion yield him a richer return than in control, mastery, and consecration of sex energy. It is a means to achievement in any definite direction. The marvel is that as consciousness of internal strength and power develops, the physical sign disappears. The peace that follows is the peace of power.

Understanding the law that all naturally and inherently is good, no base or ignoble thoughts of the reproductive functions can ever enter the mind. The growth, development, and ripening of the human seed becomes a sweet and sacred mystery, and may be studied as a science with the same pleasure, and the same purity of thought, with which one studies plant life and all its revelations.

One finds that nature has no secrets that ever need be withheld. A striking analogy is seen in the seed cradled in the pod, the birdling in its nest, and the incipient human life lovingly protected in the mother's organism. By this pure ideal a profound reverence for all of nature's mysteries and unfathomable secrets is developed; a conservation of energies is accomplished; while through the baptizing consecration of thought, the generative organs are redeemed from the desecration of the past, and their powers and functions justly and wisely appropriated.

This conservation of power is both possible and effective for the unmarried. Through love, training, and self-control, however, the married may not only attain the same conservation and appropriation, but also by the union of the spiritual forces of their two souls, greatly augment them. Love is the fulfillment of the law. Sexual love is its highest expression on the earth-plane, and sexual union is symbolical of this love. It stands as evidence of creative energy in action. Love is the impelling power, and as through affinity and attraction a chemical union takes place between two substances producing another substance, so a union of the sexes on the spiritual plane accomplishes results greater than could be accomplished separately. The artist has visions of new creations, the author has inspirations for new works, the inventor has new plans and models for machinery and devices. There is no limit to the power of a true soul union. It specifically increases the gift of healing and may be purposely directed to free a friend from pain and suffering.

The sexual union which is planned and controlled becomes glorified through conscious appropriation, while new meanings and new powers are given to conjugal love. This conservation, furthermore, is a precursor and preparation for parenthood; for the conception of welcome and desired offspring that shall in turn have the inheritance of loving intention and premeditated wisdom.

As the creative potency of man becomes understood, and as this knowledge is applied, men and women will grow in virtue, in love, in power, and will gladly and naturally devote this power to the world's interests and development.

CHAPTER 2

Karezza

Whatsoever things are true, whatsoever things are
honest; whatsoever things are just, whatsoever things are
pure, whatsoever things are lovely, whatsoever things are
of good report; if there be any virtue, and if there be any
praise, think on these things.

Karezza signifies "to express affection in both words and actions," and while it fittingly denotes the union that is the outcome of deepest human affection—love's consummation—it is used technically throughout this work to designate a controlled sexual relation.

Intelligent married people, possessing lofty aims in life and desiring spiritual growth and development, have it in their power so to accord their marital relations as to give an untold impetus to all their faculties. This is given through the act of copulation when it is the outgrowth of the expressions of love, and is at the same time completely under the control of the will.

The ordinary, hasty, spasmodic method of cohabitation, for which there has been no previous preparation and in which the wife is passive, is alike unsatisfactory to husband and wife. It is deleterious both physically and spiritually. It has in it no consistency as a demonstration of affection and is frequently a cause of estrangement and separation.

Karezza so consummates marriage that, through the power of will and loving thoughts, the crisis is not reached, but a complete control by both husband and wife is maintained throughout the entire relation—a conscious conservation of creative energy.

The law of Karezza dictates thoughtful preparation, even for several days previous to the union. Lover-like attentions and kindly acts prophesy love's appointed consummation. These bind heart to heart and soul to soul. There should be a course of training to exalt the spiritual and subordinate the physical. This is accomplished through reading and meditation. The reading should lead to exaltation of spirit and to the knowledge of the power and source of life. The authors chosen should be illuminated souls, such as Browning, Emerson, Carpenter. It is not easy to advise for individual cases. W. F. Evans, Henry Wood, and R. W. Trine have revealed the law of spirit and given practical helps in life's adjustment.

The meditation should be an act of giving up of one's will, one's intellectual concepts, to allow free usurpation of cosmic intelligence. In obedience to law, common or finite consciousness listens to cosmic consciousness. Daily, hourly, the listening soul awakens to new ideals.

At the appointed time, without fatigue of body or unrest of mind, accompany general bodily contact with expressions of endearment and affection, followed by the complete but quiet union of the sexual organs. During a lengthy period of perfect control, the whole being of each is merged into the other and an exquisite exaltation experienced. This may be accompanied by a quiet motion, entirely under subordination of the will, so that the thrill of passion for either may not go beyond a pleasurable exchange. Unless procreation is desired, let the final propagative orgasm be entirely avoided.

With abundant time and mutual reciprocity, the interchange becomes satisfactory and complete without emission or crisis. In the course of an hour, the physical tension subsides, the spiritual exaltation increases, and not uncommonly visions of a transcendent life are seen and consciousness of new powers experienced.

Before and during the time, there may be some devotional exercises, or there may be a formula of consecration of an uplifting character in which both unite. This aids in concentration and in removing the thoughts from merely physical sensations. The following has been helpful to many: "We are living spiritual beings; our bodies symbolize soul union, and in closest contact each receives strength to be more to the other and more to all the world."

This method of consummating the marriage relation is erroneously called in *Tokology*, "Sedular Absorption." Many scientists now believe there is no seed fluid secreted except through the demand of the final act of ejection. If this be true, in Karezza there is no seed to be absorbed, as under the direct control of the will, the act ceases short of the seed secreting period.

One writer called it "Male Continence," but it is no more male than female continence; to secure the greatest good, the husband and wife equally conserve their forces under a wise control; besides, "Continence" has long been erroneously accepted as the term for abstinence from the physical relation except for procreation.

Karezza is a symbol of the perfect union of two souls in marriage; it is the highest expression of mutual affection, and gives to those practicing it revelations of strength and power. It must be experienced upon a higher plane than the merely physical and may always be made a means of spiritual unfoldment. This should, indeed, be called a spiritual rather than a physical companionship. With a due reverence for the deeper meanings of the association, union and soul development are sought rather than fleeting, passional gratification.

Karezza gives to the sexual relation an office entirely distinct from the propagative act, a high office in individual development and formation of character. It is both a union on the affectional plane and a preparation for the best possible conditions for procreation.

Karezza should always be the outcome, the emblem of the deeper emotions; both husband and wife should hope and expect that the union will contribute to their spiritual growth and development. The marriage bond has given the sex functions a special consecration. In each union under spiritual law, this consecration is renewed. There is no defilement or debasement in the natural and controlled expression of sexual love.

Karezza does not lead to asceticism or repression, but rather to appropriation and expression. In acknowledging the life source and conscientiously devoting the creative principle to achievement, to the activities and purposes of life, one is put in possession of new powers and possibilities.

The time and frequency of Karezza can be governed by no certain law. Experience, however, has proven that it is far more satisfactory to have at least an interval of two to four weeks, and many find that even three or four months afford greater impetus to power and growth as well as more personal satisfaction; during the interval the thousand and one lover-like attentions give reciprocal delight, and are an anticipating prophecy of the ultimate union. According to the law of Karezza, the demand for physical expression is less frequent, for there is a deep soul union that is replete with satisfaction and is lasting. As a symbol it embodies all the manifestations of conjugal love. In all departments of life, symbols become less necessary as one develops spiritually. So in this relation, one may possibly outgrow the symbol. But both growth and satisfaction are attained through altruistic desires and through the mutual recognition and response by husband and wife to the innermost nature of each the higher self.

Be patient and determined; the reward will come in happy, united lives, in the finding of the kingdom of heaven in your own hearts, through obedience to law.

Spencer said truly, "When any law works to the advantage of the human race, then human nature infallibly submits to it, since obedience to it becomes a pleasure to man." Yes, the pleasure is in obedience, for all our sufferings come from ignorance of the law of being and failure of adjustment to that law.

Men and women should be as willing to learn the law of sex expression as they are to study; any other science of life, or any law of nature. It should not only be an intellectual study, but should be a study of experience and adjustment. In Karezza this expression and adjustment are so largely personal that special rules cannot be given, but those seeking the highest development will soon establish suitable conditions.

CHAPTER 3

Attainment Possible

It is the spirit that quickeneth;
the flesh profiteth nothing.

No doubt if the idea of Karezza is new, the first thought will be that it is impossible, and that no one can so control his life as thus proposed. But scores of married men and women attest that such self-control is perfectly and easily possible.

At all times, to subordinate the physical senses and desires to the spiritual is a matter of education and growth in the knowledge of the laws of being—a knowledge of the power of the spiritual nature.

There is no part of the body that is not under the dominion of the mind and that cannot be influenced by intelligent voluntary mental action. Certain physiological processes and muscular movements that ordinarily have been classed in voluntary are really carried on by the unconscious or subconscious action of the mind, by the intelligent operation of creative energy.

The body cannot think, cannot move, cannot perpetuate itself. It is made up of solids, fluids, and gases, and without mind it has no power; it has no living, moving, breathing, creating force in itself.

Creative energy as intelligence enables us to breathe, day in and day out, sleeping or waking. Mind in its unerring and subconscious action propels the heart's blood through radiating channels and microscopic tubes, defying the law of gravitation and keeping a uniform rhythm, day and night, for scores of years.

It is mind, surely, that enables cells to discriminate and take from heterogeneous varieties of food, and appropriate with an orderly and unerring skill material for either bone, muscle, or sinew.

All physiological functions and vital processes can be modified by a conscious action of the intellect, a voluntary mental effort. This is true of the liver, the kidneys, the skin, and the processes of digestion, circulation, excretion, and secretion. They are not automatic and fixed beyond our control, as has been taught.

One breathes naturally about twenty times a minute, but by a very little effort one may train the subconscious mind, so unceasingly engaged in inspiration and expiration, to hold the breath for a long time. Although one winks unconsciously when an object flits suddenly before the vision, still consciously he can steadily hold the eye open and gaze at the same object.

Darwin mentions the case of a person who could suspend the pulsations of the heart at pleasure and of another who could move his bowels at will, accelerating their peristaltic action by thought alone. Thinking of fruit, sour and luscious, affects the salivary glands and causes the mouth to water. The thought of some stimulant or medicinal preparation has an effect similar to that of the thing itself, even if less in degree.

Many years since I had a patient to whom I had given a preparation of podophyllum for a torpid liver. Two or three powders produced the desired result. Several months afterward, he laughingly told me that he had carried one of those powders in his pocket, and whenever he thought he needed to stimulate the action of the liver, he imagined the taste and peculiar properties of the remedy, and soon was happy in having the desired result, although he still preserved the powder. This was at least a more economical procedure for the patient than for the doctor!

Medical science is coming to recognize the power of thought over all bodily functions. It is possible, too, that the laws of the mind will become so universally understood that desired action of special functions can be obtained without even carrying the remedy in the pocket.

All so-called physical sensations represent conditions of thought, or rather results and effects of thought-building, and are more or less under control of the mind's action.

Habits of thought produce and govern susceptibility to degrees of temperature, to barometric conditions, to the varied effects of food and drink. For one, sensation lays down the law of heat and cold to the nicety of a degree, while for another, certain rheumatic pains or stings predict a westerly gale or a northeastern thunder storm. Is it any glory to make thermometers and barometers of our bodies through our cultivated sensations? Will it not rather redound to one's credit if he has power of adaptation and has ceased to limit his activities through his feelings?

The body, which has been coddled and babied through the centuries, is not the living man and must not dominate him. Man is a living, spiritual being. Recognition and acknowledgment of the power of the spirit not only frees him from limitation of the senses, but gives him dominion over every faculty of the mind and function of the body.

"It is the glory of man to control himself," and the best use to make of his life is to develop and demonstrate the supremacy of the spiritual over the physical.

Only within a few years have Western people learned that they can consciously and systematically train all their powers. This training enables the possessor to attain health, strength, peace of mind, and control of body.

Karezza teaches the supreme action of the will over the sexual nature, as well as the complete appropriation of the creative energy to high aims, lofty purposes, and enduring results. In this knowledge, man is no more the machine to be buffeted by circumstance and environment; he is rather the machinist, having control of both the mechanism and the power of the bodily instrument. He recognizes in his spiritual nature—the real man—which has unlimited resources, and he claims the ability to remove self-made limitations. He enthrones his divine nature which gives dominion and mastery, and at no time does this dominion serve him with more satisfaction than in the marital relation and in making possible the attainment of Karezza.

CHAPTER 4

Health

All life in nature is perfect; man's life is no exception if he remove self-made limitations.

Karezza is strengthening and sustaining both to husband and wife because it is virtually a union of the higher selves, from which naturally there can be no reaction. As the spiritual is developed, the physical is subordinated. Whatever contributes to soul growth enhances the power to live free from the domination of the body and bodily sensations. Thus it secures harmonious physical conditions, and the spirit manifests or pictures itself through the flesh as a harmonious whole.

Especially is it necessary for the wife to be freed from the usual dread of excessive and undesired child-bearing. Fear and anxious thought, far more than bacilli or bacteria, are productive of pain, disease, and suffering. The terrors and dread of child-birth, and the horrors of undesired maternity, have been potent factors in causing the weakness and the suffering of women.

To know that childbirth is natural and that, under harmonious conditions, it is not attended by suffering, removes a great curse from the lives of women. To know that the inherent desire for maternity is to be fulfilled under the best conditions and entirely at her own command is a wonderful boon to woman.

If, on the other hand, women are resigned to the conditions that they deem unavoidable, and patiently pay in frequent childbirths what they consider the penalty of their sex, they become little more than breeding animals. They are given no time for self -development and preparation for their obligations to the fast-increasing family.

Instances are rare when women can maintain a high standard of health and strength and bear six or eight children in ten or twelve years and, at the same time, perform the combined offices of nurse, cook, laundress, seamstress, and governess. In drudgery they drag along through the days and nights, with no outlook for the future except a recurrence of similar conditions.

Every woman owes it to herself to preserve the normal elasticity of health and strength, to become enduring for all the many obligations and activities of life, so to accord all her thinking and living that increase of years will not be attended by weakness and debility. Her maturer years, on the contrary, should be filled with increasing strength and power, veritably with the health and buoyancy of youth. The "young old lady" should become the regenerated "new woman," the glory and inspiration of the coming time. This may be consummated through the aid of Karezza.

In Karezza, the husband also experiences conditions which preserve his health and natural, vital powers. Physicists have demonstrated with incontrovertible facts that it is eminently healthy to conserve the virile principle. The seminal secretion has a wonderful imminent value and, if retained, is absorbed into the system and adds enormously to man's magnetic, mental, and spiritual force. In ordinary married life, this force is constantly being wasted. Other things being equal, the man who wisely conserves is, in concentrated mental and physical power and effectiveness, like a Daniel and his companions. He builds and constructs; he is the organizer and executive head of industries; he is the orator and the inventor. He is the leader of great movements because his power is drawn from an inexhaustible storage battery.

The testes may be considered analogous to the salivary and lachrymal glands, in which there is no fluid secreted except at the demand of their respective functions. The thought of food makes the mouth water for a short time only, while the presence of the food causes an abundant yield of saliva.

It is customary for physiologists to assume that the spermatic secretion is analogous to bile, which, when once formed, must be expelled. But substitute the word "tears" for "bile," and you put before the mind an idea altogether different. Tears, as falling drops, are not essential to life and health. A man may be in perfect health and not cry once in five or even fifty years. The lachrymal fluid is ever present, but in such small quantities that it is unnoticed. Where are tears while they remain unshed? They are ever ready, waiting to spring forth when there is an adequate cause, but they do not accumulate and distress the man because they are not shed daily, weekly, or monthly. The component elements of the tears are prepared in the system, they are on hand, passing through the circulation, ready to mix and flow whenever they are needed; but if they mix, accumulate, and flow without adequate cause, there is a disease of the lachrymal glands. While there are no exact analogues in the body, yet the tears and the spermatic fluids are much more closely analogous in their normal manner of secretion and use than are the bile and the semen. Neither flow of tears nor of semen is essential to life or health. Both are largely under the control of the imagination, the emotions, and the will; and the flow of either is liable to be arrested in a moment by sudden mental action.

It is as degrading for men and boys to allow a seminal emission without rational and proper cause as it is unmanly for them to shed tears on trivial occasions. If they could know, moreover, that an uncalled for emission is a destructive waste of life material, perhaps the formation of habits of masturbation, promiscuous intercourse, and marital profligacy, with all their disastrous consequences, might be largely prevented.

The mammary gland is an apt illustration of the law of demand and supply. In its anatomical construction and physiological function, is it not analogous to the seed-producing gland of the male?

No one has ever hinted that it is essential for health that the natural lacteal fluid of the mammary gland must be continually or frequently secreted and expelled. It is not considered a "physical necessity" or a demand of nature. Indeed, the contrary opinion prevails, that an abundant flow of milk is derogative to healthful conditions. Milk flows in answer to the demand of a newborn infant, and should it come at any other time than when thus demanded, it is considered a perversion of nature and an unnecessary drain upon the system. May it not prove that the unnecessary secretion and expulsion of the semen is as great a perversion of nature? May it not also prove that erectile tissue in action is not a positive evidence of secretion in the gland?

Physiology alone proves that the practice of Karezza imparts health and strength to man. When it is known that conservation is not so much the result of retained secretions as the transmutation and transformation of vital forces, the innermost life of man, then students will cease testing the fluids with chemicals and the bodily tissue with microscope and scalpel.

Although woman has not the semen to conserve, yet equally with man she has the thrilling potency of passion that, when well directed, heals sensitive nerves, vitalizes the blood, and restores tissue. In this deeper, truer union, the very heart of Karezza, woman as well as man prevents and cures disease. Karezza has a therapeutic value not equaled by any remedy of pharmacopoeia or by any system of healing.

The natural woman knows that virtue is not sexual repression but rather expression; that coldness, inertness, and want of feeling are due to condemnation of the life that is the center and creator of all life. She has been taught shame for the most sacred relations, and especially for the sign of the power that creates off spring, but she reverses this teaching. Is a plant ashamed to bud, bloom, and bring forth fruit?

Woman must bless the source of life; she must be loyal to her trust. She must know that sex-life and sex-expression are a natural heritage that God implanted. Wisely, thoughtfully, should she seek conservation and appropriation of that which is the heart of vitality.

Men who are borne down with sorrow because their wives are nervous, feeble, and irritable have it in their power, through Karezza, to restore the radiant hue of health to the faces of their loved ones, strength and elasticity to their steps, and harmonious action to every part of their bodies. By manifestations of tenderness and endearment, the husband may develop a response in the wife through her love-nature, which thrills every fiber into action and radiates tonic to every nerve.

Men with hearts full of love and wisdom will not be slow to accord this boon to wives whom they have pledged to love and protect, thus fulfilling the marriage sacrament.

In Karezza, creative energy is transmuted into the very life of the cell, from which is developed perfect structure and tissue. The impetus to health derived from Karezza is the right of every man and woman. It is cooperative building, love being the foundation, wisdom the designer and executor. This planning and building prophesy perpetual youth, and progeny surpassing all progenitors in strength and endurance.

CHAPTER 5

Parenthood

The desire for fatherhood and motherhood is found and expressed in the sexual instinct, which in turn evinces and is the sign of creative power. Its origin is in life itself. It is the God power, and when it comes throbbing and pulsating in every nerve, in every thought and feeling, it should be recognized as such and appropriated in a God-like manner.

The power to perpetuate the life principle is from the spiritual side of life. It is a manifestation of spirit in the flesh. Body alone can not reproduce itself; the physical man cannot perpetuate himself; the physical woman cannot perpetuate herself. Reproduction is from and through spiritual life. It is creative energy manifested in flesh. Its fulfillment is in parenthood.

Parenthood, being an expression of creative principle, and being born of the spirit, need not necessarily have its sole manifestation in the procreation of children in the flesh. It can be devoted to, and expressed in, all the great interests of the world.

The inventing, creating, organizing, and systematizing qualities of the male; the patience, the carefulness, tenderness, and attention to details, indeed, the brooding care of the female—all these are greatly needed in our government, in our religious and educational institutions, in all the affairs of life.

The human craving of either father or mother for offspring may find expression in the larger, greater, and all-inclusive power of Divine love, in its devotion to some great philanthropy, or in its concentration upon some altruistic work.

Parenthood, recognized as a manifestation of the Divine in man, as the highest and noblest expression of manhood and womanhood, gives a choice of appropriation either to spiritual or physical procreation. In Karezza, this choice is under certain and wise control.

The desire for offspring is innate in the human heart; it is the natural expression of the creative principle; it is seed-bearing on the physical plane.

In my professional experience, more women have consulted me to ascertain and overcome causes of barrenness than have sought to prevent motherhood. Those denied the privileges and blessings of maternity usually have been borne down with great sorrow. Very few have yet learned that this maternal desire may be gratified on a higher plane through the procreation of thought and ideas, and thus give satisfaction to a natural instinct.

Physiology and pathology often fail to reveal the causes of barrenness, while the physician's resources and the surgeon's knife alike afford no relief. Very frequently the cause lies deeper than can be discovered by chemistry and the microscope, or remedied by probe and scalpel. The cause may lie in the occult forces, in the lack of soul or spiritual adjustment, or it may have its origin in physical excesses.

Conservation is the great secret of power; it is possible that the heart's desire for offspring may be gratified through Karezza, through wise and temperate control of the sexual impulses, a storage of life that begets life.

In Karezza, men and women attain such development and such fine spiritual perception that they know when a soul can be begotten, and with the great power resulting from continence quickly respond.

Many cases of sterility have been overcome, even by an occasional and unsystematic temperance in the physical relation. A fruitful union frequently follows long separation of husband and wife, even though they have never had children. One may expect more certain results if the relation conforms to scientific principles.

Since penning the above, a lady called, aged thirty-nine, who had been married thirteen years, without children. At last, however, her mother heart throbbed with happy anticipations. In conversation, the fact was developed that conception had taken place immediately after a lengthy separation from her husband. Seed waste was prevented and propagation was the result. Through Karezza, this seed waste can be prevented without separation, and thus the heart's longing for children be gratified.

CHAPTER 6

Control of Procreative Powers

No words can express the helplessness, the sense of
personal desecration, the despair which sinks into the heart
of a woman forced to submit to maternity under adverse
circumstances, and when her own soul rejects it.
—H. C. Wright.

Through Karezza, unsought and undesired paternity will be a thing of the past. Children that are desired will be planned for, favorable conditions will be sought, and the conception of a human being will be an occasion for the highest expression of creative power. Time, circumstances, and conditions for the best good of the parents and the child may be chosen.

The control of the fecundating power appeals especially to those mothers who are forced into frequent child-bearing, who not only suffer loss of health and strength themselves, but are overwhelmed by their inability to do justice to their children. If such mothers are rich, the little ones are turned to the pitiless care of a nurse; if poor, the children must seek their own diversion and all their activities thus lack wise direction. Alas, they are physical mothers only, lacking the unperverted and unerring maternal instinct of the lower creation.

Women instinctively long for and desire the office of motherhood. With this desire, it is natural that they should wish suitable conditions and circumstances to enable them to perform the office well, to give children a rightful inheritance and to have the sacred office honored. It is lack of these conditions for maternity that impels women to shrink from it.

Fear of suffering that frequently attends the office also causes women to dread motherhood and often has led them to use undue measures to prevent it; it is now known that suffering is not a natural consequence of child-bearing. Even on the physical plane, if women live close to the heart of nature, adopting simple habits of dress, food, and exercise, they can to a great degree prevent the pangs of childbirth. It has been proven over and over again that painless parturition is possible.

A great truth, however, has been discovered. Through a knowledge of the spiritual forces of life and the possibility of according one's life to the law governing them, one may, under all circumstances, experience health and harmony. The inference follows that the natural functions of pregnancy and parturition, aided by a knowledge of this truth, will be free from pain and disability. The very desire to realize the spiritual ideal in reproduction, together with the consecration of the reproductive functions to that ideal, tends of itself to lessen suffering.

The very young should be trained in this ideal. Girls should early have instilled into their minds reverence for all the functions in their natures pertaining to the maternal. At the approach of womanhood, a sign of the development and ripening of the ovules occurs in what is called menstruation. Girls should be taught that this is a symbol of motherhood, a sign that the ovules are being prepared for the fructifying principle. They have already learned that the ovule of flowers is found embedded in a cell to which pollen is carried from the anthers through the stigma. Thus seed germination is accomplished. Speaking plainly, it is the sexual intercourse of plant life, from which baby plants are produced.

There is such a close analogy sexually between human and plant life that it should be taught with the same freedom and reverence. Most emphatically, the young should never receive the idea of shame or debasement in connection with any natural function.

A girl should know that the highest goal of her life is reproduction. All signs pointing to this should be joyfully welcomed. The indications of womanhood are a pledge of motherhood. The inherent maternal instinct has been expressed in a fondness for dolls, foreshadowing the joys of maternity; she gladly learns that maturity gives her the possibility of its fulfillment. Women must understand that child-bearing is a natural expression of creative energy.

They and their physicians have looked upon and treated the function as a disease and ignorantly coddled and encouraged the disorders attending it. Maternity is a divinely appointed mission; to be a mother is a sacred trust. Reverencing this trust and coming into close communion with the heart of all life replaces fear and dread with joy and satisfaction. This is an agreement with nature's plan, a law of spirit. Acknowledgment of, and obedience to, this law lessens or entirely overcomes the usual sufferings of pregnancy and of parturition.

Fearing nothing, but hoping and expecting the greatest earthly felicity, women will cease to dread or to prevent child-bearing on account of the dangers attending it, for through knowledge there is nothing to fear.

For the sake, however, of the best conditions for the development and birth of the child, men and women should intelligently and consciously control the fecundating power. Every child has a right to a parentage of thoughtful preparation, to the best that can be given him. In Karezza, this right of the unborn child is fulfilled. He becomes the inheritor of love's behests and wise designs, which shape and mold his entire life and character.

It has been taught that to fulfill literally the command to "multiply and replenish" means that it is God's law to submit to chance conception. Under other similar circumstances, that which would be called an accident or incident is in the procreation of a human being called a special providence. In his undeveloped wisdom, man may provide protection and education for his child, but fail to seek an opportunity for that child's conception at a time when its protection and education can be assured.

Man takes circumstances into his own hands and accumulates a fortune for the child to inherit, but he does not give a thought to the conditions that will bequeath to that child health and wisdom to enjoy and appropriate such an inheritance.

Men and women devote their best years to education and culture, to discoveries in ethnology, language, history, and art, to the interpretation of Norse legends and Oriental myths, to the deepest philosophical and metaphysical questions, but in all this learning and wisdom not one thought is ever breathed that will give to a child an inheritance of thoughtful preparation and chosen conditions.

Men inaugurate kindergartens, schools, and colleges for postnatal training, but in no wise do they institute plans and preparations for any prenatal culture.

This lack of knowledge and instruction directly deprives children of their best birthright and is nowise consistent with the many other measures inaugurated for the protection and development of human beings. We should accord to every child the great privilege of a birth that affords the best advantage possible, and to do this, the time and occasion should be chosen for the purpose.

Karezza affords a scientific method of controlling procreation, one in which there can be no objection on account of health, and one that appeals to the reason of every thinking person.

Under wise control, unwelcome children will be unknown, and the brand of selfish desires and indulgence will no longer be impressed upon the infant mind. As future generations understand the law of spiritual growth and mastery, their children will be superior in power and achievement to any heretofore known.

Why should we not accord to a human being even greater intelligence in its parenthood, its inception and development, than is given to the propagation of animals? Have we no intelligent protest against the ordinary chance procreation? Will not love, science, and wisdom, combined with prophetic intelligence for the betterment of the race, devise and promulgate a theory of scientific reproduction?

O men of science and wisdom! Open your storehouses of knowledge, and pour it forth to supply this demand. O women with hearts full of love and intuition! Can you not tenderly lead your sisters to understand a wise and benign appropriation of their creative powers, in which the welfare of offspring shall have first consideration?

Shall not the world cease to be peopled by unloved and undesired children? Let love be the fulfillment of law, and let us have a race of men and women that will bless the wisdom and deliberation of their progenitors.

Breathe the spirit of progress into the institution of marriage, and let all strive for descendants that shall glorify the centuries to come. Through thought-force, creative energy should project itself forward in time and give our children's children a birthright of love and an inheritance more priceless than precious stones. Let us multiply the Emersons, the Savonarolas, the Catherines of Siena, for they in turn will bless the earth.

CHAPTER 7

Free Motherhood

A partnership with God is motherhood.
What strength, what purity, what self-control,
What love, what wisdom belongs to her
Who helps God fashion an immortal soul.
                                        —*Mary Wood Allen*

When in India, I visited the Naiars, a peculiar people found on the Malabar Coast and claiming to be of Brahmin descent. They have a native government, are intelligent and educated, have good schools, and their houses average better than those in other parts of India. Except two sisters who conducted a mission industrial school for girls, there were no English in this province. The great peculiarity of the Naiars is that the women are the lords of creation. In wide contrast to the condition of the other women of that country so full of inconsistencies, they are called the free women of India.

They seek their husbands, control business interests, and through them only is the descent of property.

The family and the whole fabric of society is founded upon the mother. She is the keystone of the arch, for she chooses who shall be the father of her child and bestows her worldly goods according to her desires and discretion.

She marries the man of her choice. If for any reason, however, she deems him unfit to be a husband or the father of her child, it requires no ceremony of church or state to free her from him. Her wish and word are law.

Karezza gives a free motherhood, whether in a government controlled by men or women. Karezza is a mutual relation and it removes all vestiges of the old idea of man's dominion over woman. The pleasure and benefit to be derived are hers as much as his.

The institution of marriage becomes ideal when the desire and pleasure of the wife calls forth the desire and pleasure of the husband—when a single code of ethics governs their relation. When offspring is desired, then surely it is for woman to command and man to obey.

Henry C. Wright, a noble defender of the rights of women and children, said: "Man, in begetting a child without regard to the wishes and condition of his wife, heedless of the physical and spiritual well being of his offspring, commits the greatest outrage any human being can perpetrate on another. Motherhood should be a privilege and an opportunity, not a penalty or misfortune."

When all people concede the importance and dignity of the maternal function, then they will honor and respect woman, as does Drummond in his *Ascent of Man*. He maintains: "Mothers are the chief end of creation. In plants, the mother species heads the list. Beyond the mother with her milky breast, the Creator does not go; that is his goal. In as real a sense as a factory is meant to turn out locomotives or locks, the machinery of nature in its last resort is meant to turn out mothers."

In these and various eloquent paragraphs, this man of science honors motherhood. He exclaims that love is the supreme factor in the evolution of the world and teaches that the mother, in giving birth to children, in caring for them and educating them, gives us the highest manifestation of Divine love.

We reverence the high ideals of this philosopher and esteem him for his fearlessness. Those, however, who have studied deeply into spiritual truth do not recognize great mental and spiritual differences between men and women on account of sex. Circumstances and environment have made seeming differences. The best development and the purest lives come from a full understanding and recognition of the purely spiritual or divine in man. The knowledge of the living, spiritual truth—that man has no separate existence from God—is the most potent factor in breaking down all supposed inequalities between the sexes. This gives us a new language. There is no more talk of male or female minds, male or female qualities, for all minds are from one source. Each individual includes in his characteristics both male and female principles, both the fatherhood and motherhood of God.

When men come to know that the larger experience is in the spiritual life, neither man nor woman will patter around in Chinese shoes of conventionalism or have their conduct governed by conditions as binding as Hindu caste.

This gives to woman freedom, with its basic principles in spiritual law. She realizes that the source of love, wisdom, and knowledge is infinite; that life in its fullness is hers; that the possibilities of conquest are as great as the world; and the path is as free and wide as the universe.

She finds her true self in every situation. She loses even a suspicion that anyone wishes or has the power to curtail her privileges, while her daily external life becomes a manifestation of her internal growth and exaltation.

The mother-nature, demanding the divinest helps, in the existence of the demand feels the assurance of the supply. In the desire and fulfillment of the office of maternity, her choice as to time and circumstances becomes law.

Women have demanded and received recognition in every profession and vocation; they have eloquently appealed for the duties and privileges of citizenship. In many states they have been allowed, through the ballot, a voice in adjusting disputed policies of city and country; they have been given positions of responsibility and emolument; but alas, how seldom are they accorded the freedom of choice for the fulfillment of the natural function of child-bearing.

Elizabeth Cady Stanton, after thirty years devotion to the enfranchisement of woman, said that if the ballot were granted fully and freely to women, she would have entered only the vestibule to her emancipation; and that with the conditions that love and freedom would give to her sexual life she could raise a race of gods.

Women in every station of life, from the reigning queen of the greatest nation of the earth to the humblest toiler in the hamlet; wives of men expounding the higher law from the pulpit and wives of men in slums, ignorant of all law and justice, have all alike been subjected to the inconvenience, suffering, and debasement of chance maternity. Thus the hearts of intelligent and pure-minded people have been dulled by tradition to the injustice and wrong perpetrated upon both mother and child.

Women whose intuitions have been trained to lofty purposes and aims will seek and expect the best conditions for procreation. The child in its glorified life will bless her thoughtfulness and fidelity. In freedom, the behests of love are fulfilled. Ideal parentage gives ideal children.

It belongs to institutions of learning to remove from sexual science the stigma of secrecy and prudery, and it is the privilege of enlightened womanhood to apply scientific knowledge to the conception and bearing of children; to apply the accumulated wisdom of the ages to the most responsible office of maternity. To do this she must be free to exalt her sexual life to the fulfillment of its highest mission. In this enlightenment and exaltation, the devoted husband will naturally and freely accord his conduct to her wishes. Love's commands are always founded on justice; love's obedience is willing obedience.

Happy he
"With such a mother! Faith in womankind
Beats with his blood, and trust in all things high
Comes easy to him.

CHAPTER 8

Married and Mated

It is the woman of you, and not the physical body,
which is the wife. Nature is a system of nuptials.
All exist as the offspring or product of a marriage.
—Grindon

Karezza develops a closer bond of union between husband and wife. They two are united for life; they enter the marriage relation thoughtfully, with the hope of happiness and mutual helpfulness. But what a travesty is the usual marriage upon the one idealized, not only in song and story, but in every loving heart. How soon many hearts are broken and many hopes blasted, and that mainly because the sexual relationship in marriage is instigated by selfish motives and for personal gratification.

Marriage is a man-made institution to protect nature in her plan to surround and guard individuals with restraint for the benefit of the community. Marriage is the one morally conceded and legally recognized form of association of one man with one woman, granting the rights and privileges of the sexual relation as husband and wife.

Men and women begin married life without a true estimate of the relation to be sustained. They do not realize that all conduct of life in its bearings and results, depends upon a law deeper in its fundamental principles and more nearly just in its execution, than any human law. Marital unhappiness is caused chiefly by ignorance of the psycho-physiological laws governing the relations between the sexes and ignorance of what is due to each from the other in all of their associations, more especially in the sexual union.

In ignorance, every couple enters marriage as a new experience. At present there is no education except that of observation, and no school except that of experience, to fit people for living together in marriage. They enter the relation, believing it to be for life; for better and not for worse. The young and inexperienced enter it tempted by love, full of energy, desire, and expectation; others, more mature in years, through a wider knowledge of the ways of the world, enter it for reasons perhaps better considered and weighed.

With few exceptions, the subjects of procreation, pregnancy, and all matters pertaining to sexual science are tabooed between the sexes previous to marriage. By the "holy banns" of the priest, the Gordian knot of secrecy is loosened. The shrinking timidity of the wife is met by a bravado of the superior knowledge of the husband. He is imbued with the belief an ironclad tradition of the ages that marriage gives him a special license. Under this license, often and often he puts to shame the prostitution of the brothel. Too frequently, alas, the sweet flower of love is blighted forever.

The day of wedding bells, of blooming exotics and friendly congratulations, ends in a night of suffering and sorrow. The love must be strong and deep that can withstand selfish gratification, especially if the gratification be for only one and that at the expense, pain, and disappointment of the other.

Lift the veil of secrecy from these subjects, and study sexual science with greater care and devotion than is given to furnishing the cottage in which you expect to live. No better thing can be done to cement lives in the promised union and to insure the hoped-for happiness.

True marriage is based upon that recognition of the individuality of both husband and wife which brings voluntary, not compelled, cooperation in all the departments of family life. Only when souls flowing together, acting as one, distinct in individuality but united in their action, are thus mated are the psycho-physiological laws met and satisfied.

"Whosoever looketh on a woman to lust after her hath committed adultery." Tolstoy says: "These words relate not only to the wife of another, but especially to one's own wife. Woman, in bringing a child into the world and giving it her bosom, sees clearly that her affairs are more serious than those of man. Consequently woman is necessarily superior to man. She becomes superior by the acts of generation, birth, and nursing."

Painful recitals of unwritten annals of the lives of those who endure in silence or seek relief through the courts from the wrongs inflicted upon them would fill volumes. Better knowledge of the relations between husband and wife would avoid these conditions. There are earnest, intelligent people today who have come to believe that marriage can be lifted to a plane of spiritual companionship far exceeding any pleasure known to the merely physical.

There can be no true marriage unless attraction, affinity, and harmony first exist in the soul. True union, indeed, depends on a psychic law, and its permanence upon the spiritual element that pervades it.

The clerk's certificate, the wedding ring, the priest's blessing, cannot make two individuals husband and wife. This ceremony is only proof to the world of the heart union already existing. It is an institution honored by law and custom for developing family life.

If love is the keynote of the union of husband and wife, a harmonious adjustment of their daily lives and conduct is possible, for love is the embodiment of intelligence and meets every condition with boundless tact and wisdom.

Love teaches that no man owns his wife, that no woman owns her husband, that in no wise can the marriage bond be construed into owner ship. Love makes obedience lighter than liberty. Individual habits, individual tastes, and individual desires are recognized and respected. "I will" and "you must" are not in love's vocabulary. The one act symbolizing union and affection, giving expression to creative life, by love's enactment, is born of desires that are mutual and participated in with equal pleasure.

The truly married consummate this union with perfect freedom and naturalness. At the same time, their hearts leap with joy as they awake to the deeper meanings of life.

The blending of the two in sexual consummation is fulfillment of law as much as is the union of the fructifying principle in plants. Sexual instinct is not something to be killed, to be ignored, to be stamped out of existence. Man is not to become an ascetic, but rather he is to consider this sign a confirmation of his deeper relation to the entire universe, and to know that a right appropriation of the sex-force is required. Creative energy is neither for one moment to be stultified nor considered ignoble.

In Karezza, they give willing obedience to love's commands, and in this union the entire nature of husband and wife blend in a communion that is fraught with calmness, self-control, justice, and altruism. Each abides in the love of the other; each gives and each receives.

Reciprocity is the basis for the ethics of marriage. To give and to receive are equally virtuous. Upon this fundamental principle the success of Karezza depends—one calls, and the other responds; by a mutual understanding and a mutual participation, the selfish element is ruled out, and every consummation of passion becomes a true marriage sacrament, which reflects upon character all that is permanent and valuable.

It gives to marriage a significance that is exalted as much above the ordinary union as human life is higher than animal life.

In abstinence except for procreation, one propagates only, while Karezza conduces to the building of character and spiritual growth, and at the same time the sexual functions are honored, refined, and dignified. In this marriage, there is no bondage for either man or woman; it is a result of the recognition of the spiritual nature of man, and in this recognition he is enabled so to order his life that he is master of conditions. He causes the world of matter to serve him. He not only claims and appropriates the forces of nature, but in his new strength and power, in his knowledge of the all-potent spiritual forces, he breaks the bonds of supposed fleshly limitations. In the wisdom of spiritual knowledge, he acquires the conscious ability to divert his entire nature—his thoughts, aspirations, and desires—into channels of effectiveness.

Desire should not be crushed and obliterated, as taught by the Oriental adepts and all ascetics, but rather, wisely directed and appropriated.

Desire is the prophecy of attainment. There can be no growth without it. Desire is the germ that bursts the chrysalis of inheritance and tradition; it gives wings to the spirit, aiding it to overcome bodily disabilities, and to break the clanking chains of erroneous thinking. Guided and guarded by intellect and intuition, it leads to knowledge of higher truths. Desire to drink from the source of life, love and intelligence enables one to experience an at-one-ment with universal principle itself.

"Seek and ye shall find." Through desire, marriage may be glorified, and those joined together in the highest law cannot be put asunder by any misstatements or misjudgments of men and women, nor by their own trivial errors committed in ignorance.

Each comes to know the soul of the other in its perfectness and knows only to love and to honor. The love and loyalty pledged on the wedding day are nothing as compared to the love and loyalty of an open vision. The abiding happiness fulfills the promise of the past.

In peace and reverence, marriage becomes a holy bond of matrimony, a more enduring bond than can be conferred by prince, potentate, or state. Each bears to the other a noble allegiance, not as a fetter but as a garland.

If I could present a composite photograph of the correspondence from my files, the burden of which is the secret tyranny of unrestrained passion over the lives of men and women, it would form a marvelously strong appeal to science to come to the relief of the ignorant. Not infrequently several children are born within fifteen or eighteen months of each other, from one mother, while motherhood, in its manifold functions, presents no plea to command restraint and respect from the husband. For the relief of such mothers, and to prevent similar experiences, I dip my pen in the fire of love to write. While pleading for the freedom of women and justice to children, I do not forget that man commits the wrong in ignorance. Although his heart is full of love and a desire to bless the woman of his choice, he has never been instructed in the way. Simply and blindly has he followed the example and guidance of men, equally ignorant, and accepted the traditions of man's necessities and woman's compulsory obedience.

Most men are true to their social, religious, and political opinions, and once seeing and understanding a better way of life, they will give loyal allegiance to nobler ethics in marriage.

A mother in the far West writes:

I was a school teacher in Illinois, and was married at twenty-two, ten years ago. I came with my husband to make a home in a new country. We endured many privations, but none so great as the separation from friends and congenial society. The burden of child-bearing, so far from dear mother and relatives, the days and nights of agonizing fear, of anxious watching over little ones, of physical suffering, and, most of all, heart anguish, cannot be told. Dare I, can I write of my husband, he whom I adored, he who has shared his all with me? Does a man love a woman when he is not just to her? Must I stifle the cry in my heart for some response to my deeper nature?

Would death be any relief? But I put back all thoughts of death when I feel the searching trust of six pairs of eyes and Harry. One thing, dear friend, I have never contemplated, is leaving him; but alas, my own bitter experience shows me what is revealed in the divorce courts; and tell me, tell me truly, is this wrong and injustice sanctioned by God and nature?

Can a man be virtuous who makes nightly demands on a woman that loathes and repulses his embrace; when either sickness or even pregnancy is scarcely considered a barrier? Must I continue bearing children that we cannot clothe and educate properly, and most of all, that are not born of love and desire; whose first cry seems like a wail of protest against a chance existence?

Do I weary you? I beg and plead that you may not spurn my letter unless you can give no hope, for in all the wide world there is no other to whom I dare go.

Hopefully and sincerely,
Dora S.

My reply was as follows:

Dear Dora S.:

Every graveyard is filled with monuments of experiences like yours. Dear heart, I believe there is help and salvation for you. You have given me a glimpse of your deep, abiding love for your husband, and it is through this and your ability to give him your confidence that you will find help. If he will listen to you at all, you may yet enjoy a true marriage on earth. I send you the *Better Way* by Newton. I also wish to know if you have ever heard that intercourse may be had without culmination, no emission being allowed? This naturally gives perfect control of the fecundating power. Many people practice this method and claim the highest possible enjoyment and no loss of vitality. Your intelligence and desire will lead you to accord your lives to this latter method that has been both light and help to many others. You will, I am sure, be freed from this bondage to passion. It is a matter of control to which every person can train himself, and a road in which the intelligent are easily led. If I can serve you farther, please command me.

Sincerely,
A. B. S.

Nearly a year afterward, I received the following letter:

Dear Dr. Stockham:

I did not intend so long a time to elapse before letting you know of my deep, heartfelt gratitude for your timely advice. I could repay you in no better way than to cite my experience for the benefit of others who suffer as I did, and who from unselfish motives desire and seek relief.

When I received your letter, I read it at once to Harry. With a tone of impatience, he said, "That is a woman's idea."

That night and days following, we were both thoughtfully silent. When I had read the *Better Way*, I asked him to peruse it, saying to him: "Here is a man's idea of marriage. He seems to be a man of intelligence and one whose opinion should command respect from those desiring to live aright. He, though a man, puts greater restrictions on conduct than the woman idea does."

"For you, Dora, I will read it, but you must not be too sure that I will accept any new-fangled notions," he replied.

The book certainly interested him, for he did not retire until it was finished. The babe had been restless, and though he knew I had not slept, he never spoke a word. Days and nights passed, and the subject was not broached. I felt that I had done my part, and it was for him to speak.

It came over me with an inexpressible horror that, in according our lives to Newton's theory, he felt, I was exercising a tyranny and coercion even greater than I had suffered. It had never occurred to me that Harry might think I was assuming a dictatorial attitude in the matter, for I preferred his fullest and most cordial cooperation in that relation from which he would gain equally with me. Still, I could not tell; he was attentive, often planning surprises for my comfort and happiness, unusually patient and kind with the children, but in the long days and nights never a word of love and trust.

I recalled having once heard that "absence is the best test of affection." So I planned an inexpensive trip, and with my two youngest children visited a cousin twenty-five miles away.

We—Harry and I—had never been separated for even one night in almost eleven years. We soon discovered that ours was a real soul union, and that we had committed the greatest desecration by sacrificing this union to such frequent physical embraces. Absence and the silent messenger of love, the written page, enabled us to open our hearts to each other. The long letters that followed were a renewal of courtship days, only our love seemed more sacred and hallowed by consecration to better purposes.

I must not take your time to tell you all, but you will be glad to know that we have adopted the "woman's idea" and found it far from difficult. It seems almost strange to ourselves, but weeks often elapse without any sign of physical demand, and we are far happier in this new life than in the old.

Harry joins me in gratitude to you.

Very sincerely,
Dora S.

Thus many, many testify that the physical union under a wise, intellectual control leads to a true spiritual marriage, out of which develops the looked-for and expected happiness in this relation.

In obedience to the law of Karezza, satiety is never known, and the married are never less than lovers; each day reveals new delights, each hour is an hour of growth, the entire life blossoms in joy and revels in golden fruitage. The common daily sarcasms of married people are at an end, the unseemly quarrels have no beginnings, and the divorce courts are cheated of their records. Welcome children are born of the spirit and develop in a beneficent atmosphere of trust and harmony. The ideal family, living in mutual love and helpfulness, magnifies the law and stands as an emblem of purity and truth.

CHAPTER 9

Procreation of Thought

*As far as we yet know, spirit or mind is the substance,
it shows through the body—is served by the body.*
—Koradine

In Karezza, the procreation of thought is possible. Spirit is
the ego, the higher self, the Divine principle in man that
expresses his unity with all nature. The reader will
remember that soul is spirit in action. Soul is the "spiritual
body" mentioned by Saint Paul; it bears a more intimate
relation to the physical body than a hand does to a glove.

In the soul, all the activities of our being are impelled.
The movement of muscles, the processes of digestion and
nutrition—all occur as manifestations of the spiritual or
soul nature. It is in the soul that we find the senses and
emotions. The soul also has the power of choice and the
ability to fashion character. Every soul has a dual nature,
the masculine and feminine; intellect and wisdom
characterizing the male, intuition and affection the female.
These exist to some degree in every human being. Grindon
says: "All that belongs to thought, understanding, or mind
is masculine; all that belongs to will, intuition, or affection
of heart is feminine.

When one acts immediately from the intellectual
principle, manliness is foremost; when from the will

principle, womanliness. The most consistent, perfect personality is that in which both the male and the female principles are harmoniously developed. Since sex is of the soul, is it not possible that as spiritual unity develops thought may be procreated? That would mean a procreation on the spiritual plane of ideas and theories to be practically developed for the good of the world.

The physical relation may or may not be of value for this higher procreation. It has been proven, however, that in the Karezza relation the creative principle becomes active in both husband and wife. While the spiritual senses are thus attuned to the finest perception in soul vibration, ideas of great moment are conceived. It is within the power of men and women, interested in the operation of spiritual law, further to demonstrate the validity of the theory.

Newton says: "It is important to know that there are other uses for the procreative element than the generation of physical offspring, far better uses than its waste in momentary pleasure. It may, indeed, be better wasted than employed in imposing unwelcome burdens on toil-worn and outraged women. But there should be no waste. This element, when retained in the system, may be coined into new thoughts, perhaps new inventions, grand conceptions of the true, the beautiful, the useful; or into fresh emotions of joy, and impulses of kindness and blessing to all around. This is, in fact, but another department of procreation. It is the procreation of thoughts, ideas, feelings of goodwill, intuitions of truth—that is, it is procreation on the mental and spiritual planes, instead of physical. It is just as really a part of the generative function as is the begetting of physical offspring. It is by far the greater part; for physical procreation can ordinarily be participated in but seldom, while mental and spiritual procreation may and should go on through all our earthly lives, yea, through all our immortal existence."

To the mature man, a consecration of virile powers is essential to the maintenance of a high tone of vitality and of manly vigor. On it depends the degree of positive or impregnative force which characterizes the individual in his mental activities.

A speaker or writer who is addicted to waste in this department, though he may talk and write with great profuseness, may expect that his words will be comparatively powerless in their effect upon others. They will lack germinating power. But he who conserves this element in a calm, deliberate union, charges not only his words, but the very atmosphere with a power which penetrates and begets new thoughts and new emotions in those whom he addresses.

"Every idea is an intellectual child, and if it be a pleasant thing to have physical sons and daughters, what are the power, the opulence, the enjoyments of him who abounds in ideas, the beautiful and immortal sons and daughters of the soul?"

Who, then, are the true old bachelors and old maids, and who the really childless? Not so much the unmarried by ring and book, as they who have not courted and wedded nature, receiving from her in reply a family of beautiful ideas.

He is a spiritual parent who has learned to drink from the well of truth, and from the deep resources of his being, has discovered the secret powers of life. In outward manifestation he may preach, teach, heal and prophesy, but should he sit quietly in his own home, his life is a silent benediction to all, even to those who do not come into his presence. His creative energy brings forth according to the potent power of thinking. Through the contagion of thought his influence has infinite possibilities.

Spiritual pleasures transcend those of a physical nature, and all practices that lead one to walk in the paths of light and truth conduce to peace and harmony. Not only this, but through the laws that govern the occult forces in the practice of Karezza, there are more far-reaching results than accrue to the individual in the ordinary sexual relation.

Laboulaye long ago asserted: "The passions take the place in the soul which the will does not occupy, and there may yet be discovered a process by which passion may be transmuted into intellectual fiber. This is, indeed, the last and highest possibility of human culture."

People will know this place, the functions of passion, and their relations to the will when they understand the germinating power of thought and have their sexual life under a wise control. Men and women practicing Karezza attest that their very souls in union take on a procreating power, and that it seems to have an impregnating force far transcending in power and intelligence any ordinary thought-force. These mighty soul-conceptions demand generation and birth, for the world is in need of their regenerating power. Let all children of men listen for these messages. Let them go into the hush of the spirit and wait in the night stillness for the revelation. It may come in the fire of a poet or the eloquence of an orator, but certainly if souls are attuned to life's harmonies, the law will be fulfilled in song and prophecy.

This silence is not mere silence of sound, but even thought is hushed, the eyes forget to see, and the ears forget to hear; only spirit listens to spirit. It is as Koradine describes when Tommy was healed: "Then came a deep, deep stillness that cleansed and hushed all thought, for there was no need of thought, no room for speech; just stillness, stillness."

In this ecstatic stillness the problems of the philanthropist are solved; the sculptor's marble glows with life; the painter's canvas reflects love and intelligence; while the desires of each are lifted to the highest and truest expressions of the soul, expressions that shall hasten the universal brotherhood of man.

CHAPTER 10

Spiritual Growth

I well perceive how in thine intellect already shines the eternal light, which, once seen, always kindles love.
—Dante

Souls really united progress unitedly. This is the strongest and greatest argument for this altruistic union. The highest aim in life should be spiritual development and the attainment of power and strength in this direction. Habits and conditions that contribute to this should be sought.

Miller says: "With Zugassent's Discovery [Karezza] comes also the one supreme truth, that its greatest crown of honor consists in its conducing to the highest and noblest spiritual development."

What is spiritual development? It is coming into recognition of the supremacy of the spiritual over the physical; it is conscious mastery in one sense, and in another it is a knowledge of the God-like in man that takes possession of him, leading and guiding him in all the walks of life.

It is true that in Karezza one experiences growth in the spiritual nature. This is attained through the habit of self-control and mastery, and through the desire of each for the best good of the other, and to the high aspirations accompanying the relation. Once having experience in

Karezza, one will never return to the ordinary habits in which sensuality and selfishness so often predominate.

All spiritual experience is growth in the knowledge of man's divinity, of his inseparable union with the omnipresent principle of life. He may come to a sudden awakening of this great truth of his being which results in an instantaneous conversion, like Saul of Tarsus, or it may more slowly dawn upon his perception as in the case of Saul of old as he listened to the divine harmonies of David's harp.

Whenever and however man perceives this truth, it is borne upon his inner consciousness that the real enduring things of life belong to the spirit, while the evanescent, fleeting, unstable things are material. He comes to rule his life according to this knowledge, and although he lives in the world, he is not of it, and all things present new meanings to him.

In no part of life's domain are these new meanings more clearly perceived than in the reproductive powers. In the loving companionship of husband and wife, in the conception and birth of spiritual and physical offspring in all their innermost relations, their lives are attuned to nature's harmonies, their very existence vibrates with the divine unity of the universe.

Both men and women can train this creative energy into power. The word is the sword of the spirit. It is a well proven law that the reiteration of a thought brings about a condition which makes manifest what the thought expresses. Therefore, let one repeat again and again: "I am a creator, not merely of human children, but a creator of thoughts, of ideas, and of resources. I devote my great heart-love to the interests of the world. There is no task too onerous for my devotion, no service too difficult for my undertaking. All children are mine, all interests are mine. Gladly and cheerfully do I answer the call to serve those who need me. I am both father and mother. In joy and gladness do I consecrate myself to the world."

In this prayer of faith and fulfillment, one recognizes the power of the omnipotent creative life principle, and in beneficence and freedom experiences a vivifying stimulus to works of love.

Here is given a glimpse of the greatest spiritual law yet discovered. It is a key to self- training for power and mastery. It is power itself. This theory is not based upon denials and the asceticisms of all religious teachings of the past. Oriental philosophers and western theologians have usually united in counseling people to kill out desire and passion. The nirvana of existence and the sanctification of saints are alike to be beyond ambition and desire. On the contrary, the philosophy of today expounds a law of affirmation in which one attains development of the self in power, together with a systematic consecration of all aspirations and faculties.

We are living, spiritual beings. Claiming this, we enter consciously into our possessions, understanding that we have creative powers born of the spirit. By wise appropriation of them we become superior to bodily conditions, until they wheel into line and serve us. We become greater than anything with which we have to deal. We enthrone the ego, which is spirit, and utilize something of the divine potency which has been hidden by human limitations and erroneous thinking. Man has been bound by ignorance, but he comes through development and spiritual consciousness to know his power.

As God, life and law become synonymous in the student's mind, physical and spiritual science join hands in demonstrating the problems of existence.

No wider field of exploration is presented to the discoverer of nature's secrets than that of marital ethics. Groveling in the darkness of ignorance and superstition, man has hitherto closed to himself the doors of investigation in this province, labeling them unclean. Hence forth purity guards the entrance, and wisdom demands that youth shall not be deprived of the benefits of the experience of those who have knowledge to give. Instead of associating creative life and energy with things base and un clean, man will set all his thoughts to words as bright and enduring as the stars, and they will be the light, love and intelligence that guide his feet.

If we can perceive beauty in everything of God's doings
we may argue that we have reached
the true perception of universal law.
—*Ruskin*

Testimony of a Young Lady Missionary
The following correspondence was originally published in "Creative Life," a brochure for young ladies. It is reproduced here as especially corroborative of the theories advanced on pages 14–18 and 109, and no doubt will be read with interest and profit:

Dear Dr. Stockham:

When I read your great book *Tokology* and looked at your portrait, for the first time in my life I felt that I had found one in whom I could confide, and from whom I might hope for real help.

Very early in life I became addicted to a bad, secret habit. It does not seem as if I ever learned it. I seemed always to have had it; nor did I know I was doing wrong until about eighteen years of age, when my conscience seemed to tell me it was not right. I was a professing Christian, and I began to feel that any secret propensity, no matter what the pleasure it gave, could not be right.

Sometime after I read of the fearful results that would follow this habit, I soon decided that I must stop. I made up my mind to conquer the habit solely by my own will power, but utterly failed. Humbled, I sought Divine help; but for a long time it seemed that to stop the sun in his course would prove as easy a task as to abandon the habit entirely.

At twenty-two, a year after graduating, I went out to China as a missionary. For more than two years I realized what it was to be kept by the power of God; but like many a drunkard, I began to think I was safe and neglected to be as watchful and prayerful as I should have been, and, being overtaken by temptation, yielded several times. The desire is still there, and what I want to know is this:

What course of treatment will succeed in destroying the desire?

Should I entertain the idea of marriage?

What effect will the past have upon the marriage relation?

I do not expect to be married for a year or more. My intended husband is also a missionary. I am in perfect health, but have a poor memory. I take frequent baths and live an abstemious life. Please advise me at ———. If you can offer relief, I shall always be

Gratefully yours,
C.

To this earnest appeal I sent this reply:

Dear Miss C.:

I thank you most sincerely for your confidence. There certainly must be help for you as you so greatly desire it. I think you would not have had such a struggle if you had understood that passion is simply the evidence or sign of creative power. It does not follow that this creative power should be devoted to procreation, but it may be used in any good work. Now, according to your attitude of mind will be your experience. When the feeling comes on, say: "Yes, I know I am a creator. What am I to do?" It may be to form plans, help another, to teach school, to build a home, or what ever comes before you in your life work. Respond quickly. At once think out your plans, create, and lo, what you call temptation is gone. It is a call from God. Do you know we are wrong in attaching baseness to these feelings? Get that idea out of your mind.

The treatment most surely lies in following the law. Turn your creative power to good uses, to tremendous uses, if need be. Your consecration to good work is all right, now consecrate especially your creative powers. Every indication of passion must be treated as a call from God for some new work some creation. Put your mind to work to know what it is.

It is not the body that calls; it is the spirit, and obedience is the cure.

Say over and over again, "I am a creator. What am I to produce?" Listen, listen, and God will answer.

Yours sincerely,
A. B. S.

No letter ever gave me such real joy as her answer. Believing that the perusal of it will be helpful to many, I quote with the writer's permission:

Dear Doctor:

Your letter was received several weeks ago when I was away on a tour speaking at missionary meetings.

Really, I do not know when I have been at such a loss for words as I am in finding any that will correctly and sufficiently express my gratitude for what you have done for me.

For a long time I have thought that the work of the Christian physician is such a noble one that it is second only to that of the Christian minister and missionary. Since receiving your letter, it has seemed as though I might go farther than that and place it before that of the Christian ministry; but perhaps it would be more nearly correct to feel that, in your particular case, both offices are combined, for who could better minister to the soul, or teach a spiritual truth, of more vital importance than you have done in my case?

As I read and re-read that part of your letter in relation to the cure, and began to comprehend its full meaning and bearing, I felt as I have done at important crises of my life when some new spiritual truth has fully dawned upon me, and I have taken a great stride in the Christian life, and my feeling towards you was more than that of gratitude and admiration. You have done me good for life, as you have done many others, and who knows how much good to future generations?

Were I to send you five times the amount you charged, you would be no more nearly paid for what you have done for me than by the amount named. I take the knowledge gained as a gift from God, through you His agent, realizing that thereby my responsibility is increased and knowing that from Him you will receive your reward.

All being well, I shall be married at home in August and return at once to China. I may go by Chicago. If I should do so, it would be a very great gratification to me to have the honor of meeting you and the privilege of thanking you in person for what you have done for me.

Sincerely yours,
C.

The following is from a personal friend, eminent as a teacher of metaphysical philosophy:

I thank you, dear doctor, for the perusal of *Karezza* in manuscript. God bless you—I know it is true. I have had experience that has proved it to my satisfaction. To me the experience is very sacred, but if it aids to lift the veil (or chain) of animalism from the hearts of women and men and thus open the realm to spiritual possibilities, I have no objection to your using it. . . .

My wife and I had for months talked over together this problem with its possible results. With our deep love for each other, and our love and interest for humanity, we wished no theory to be left unproven.

Each of us had made a close study of the Science of Being, so we well understood the power of thought, and knew that the mind must con sent before the simplest act in life can be per formed. This was our theory: Man and woman are opposite to and counterpart of each other, as Tennyson beautifully expresses it:

For woman is not undeveloped man,
But diverse—

Not like to like, but like in difference,
Yet in the long years liker must they grow;
The man be more of woman, she of man;
He gain in sweetness and in moral height,
She mental breadth,
Till at last she set herself to man,
Like perfect music unto noble words;
Self -reverent each and reverencing each,
Distinct in individualities,
But like each other ev'n as those who love.
Then comes the statelier Eden back to man;
Then reign the world's great bridals, chaste and calm;
Then springs the crowning race of humankind.
May these things be!"

So then we said that man might fully appreciate woman, and that woman might fully appreciate man. To do this, it is necessary that they adjust themselves on a spiritual plane, that he may be more a woman in nature and she more a man, and yet maintain the secret of their individuality. . . .

To make the experiment complete, for several successive cohabitations we kept the physical under complete control at no time allowing a crisis.

We found that neither of us was disturbed in any physical sense. There was no uneasiness, no unrest, no unsatisfied desire. Rather, on the contrary, the satisfaction was complete, resulting in a beautiful rest and a sweet sleep. Each occasion was indeed a sacrament.

I feel confident, however, that this particular relation could not have been satisfactory had we not known the power of the mind over the body. We were fortified and prepared for each occasion. We fixed our minds on and expected spiritual attainment. The result was perfectly successful. We had previously agreed upon the duration (the complete union not more than thirty minutes) and that there must not be a desire on the part of one which the other would not readily meet. Following the relation, side by side, in the beautiful stillness, I experienced a peace, a perfect satisfaction passing mortal understanding. I was lifted up and up. I seemed to go into the realm of spirit clairvoyant intensely so not to behold spirits, but rather spiritual possibilities. Indeed it hath not entered into the heart of man to conceive all the things prepared for him, with the proper appropriation of creative energy.

To those seeking knowledge from the spirit of truth, my name may be given. To all others I am,

Sincerely,
Sigma.
Chicago, February 8, 1896.

In "Male Continence," a pamphlet now out of print, after giving a graphic and eloquent plea for the rights of the child, the writer says:

The discovery was occasioned and even forced upon me by a very sorrowful experience. In the course of six years, my wife went through the agonies of five births. Four of them were premature. Only one child lived. This experience was what directed my studies and kept me studying. After our last disappointment I pledged my word to my wife that I would never again expose her to such fruitless suffering. I made up my mind to live apart from her, rather than break this promise. I conceived the idea that the sexual organs have a social function which is distinct from the propagative function, and that these functions may be separated practically. I experimented on this idea, and found that the self-control which it requires is not difficult; that my enjoyment was increased; that my wife's experience was very satisfactory, as it had never been before; that we had escaped the horrors and fear of involuntary propagation. This was a great deliverance. It made a happy household. I communicated my discovery to a friend. His experience and that of his household were the same. In normal condition, men are entirely competent to choose in sexual intercourse whether they will stop at any point in the voluntary stages of it, and so make it simply an act of communion, or go through to the involuntary stage, and make it an act of propagation.

The situation may be compared to a stream in three conditions, viz., (1) a fall; (2) a course of rapids above the fall; and (3) still water above the rapids. The skillful boatman may choose whether he will remain in the still water, or venture more or less down the rapids, or run his boat over the fall. But there is a point on the verge of the fall where he has no control over his course; and just above that, there is a point where he will have to struggle with the current in a way which will give his nerves a severe trial, even though he may escape the fall.

If he is willing to learn, experience will teach him the wisdom of confining his excursions to the region of easy rowing, unless he has an object in view that is worth the cost of going over the falls.

You have now our whole theory. It consists in analyzing sexual intercourse, recognizing in it two distinct acts, the social and the propagative, which can be separated practically, and affirming that it is best, not only with reference to prudential considerations, but for immediate pleasure, that a man should content himself with the social act, except when he intends procreation.

(1) It does not seek to prevent the intercourse of sexes, but rather to prevent that which generally puts an end to such intercourse. (2) It does not seek to prevent the natural effects of the propagative act, but to prevent the propagative act itself except when it is intended to be effectual. (3) Of course it does not seek to destroy the living results of the propagative act, but provides that impregnation and child-bearing shall be voluntary, and therefore desired.

And now to speak affirmatively, the exact thing that our theory does propose is to take that same power of moral restraint and self-control which Paul, Malthus, the Shakers, and all considerate men use in one way or another to limit propagation, and instead of applying it, as they do, to the prevention of the intercourse of the sexes, to introduce it at another stage of proceedings, viz., after the sexes have come together in social effusion and before they have reached the propagative crisis; thus allowing the most essential freedom of love, and at the same time avoiding undesired procreation and all the other evils incident to male incontinence.

The objection urged to this method is, that it is unnatural and unauthorized by the example of other animals. I may answer that cooking, wearing clothes, living in houses, and almost everything else done by civilized man is unnatural in the same sense, and that a close adherence to the example of the brutes would require us to forego speech and go on all fours! But, on the other hand, if it is natural in the best sense, as I believe it is, for rational beings to forsake the example of the brutes and improve nature by invention and discovery in all directions, then truly the argument turns the other way, and we shall have to confess that until men and women find a way to elevate their sexual functions above those of the brutes, by introducing into them self-control and moral culture, they are living in unnatural degradation.

But I will come closer to this objection. The real meaning of it is that it is a difficult interruption of a natural act. But every instance of self- denial is an interruption of some natural act. The man who virtuously contents himself with a look at a beautiful woman is conscious of such an interruption. The lover who stops at a kiss denies himself a natural progression. It is an easy, descending grade through all the approaches of sexual love, from the first touch of respectful friendship to the final complete amalgamation. Must there be no interruption of this natural slide? Brutes, animal, or human tolerate none. Shall their ideas of self-denial prevail? Nay, it is the glory of man to control himself, and the Kingdom of Heaven summons him to self-control in all things. If it is noble and beautiful for a betrothed lover to respect the law of marriage in the midst of the glories of courtship, it may be even more noble and beautiful for the wedded lover to respect the laws of health and propagation in the midst of the ecstasies of sexual union. The same moral culture that ennobles the antecedents and approaches of marriage will some time surely glorify the consummation.

The method of controlling propagation which results from our argument is natural, healthy and effectual.

The useless expenditure of seed certainly is not natural. God cannot have designed that men should sow seed by the wayside where they do not expect it to grow, nor in the same field where it has already been sown and is growing; and yet such is the practice of men in the ordinary sexual relation. They sow seed habitually where they do not wish it to grow. This is wasteful of life and cannot be natural.

Yet is it not manifest that the instinct of our nature demands congress of the sexes, not only for propagative, but for social and spiritual purposes? The act of propagation should be reserved for its legitimate occasions when conception is intended. The idea that sexual intercourse, limited to the social part of it, is impossible or difficult, and there fore not natural, is contradicted by the experience of many. Abstinence from masturbation is impossible or difficult where habit has made it a second nature, and yet no one will say that habitual masturbation is natural. So abstinence from the propagative part of sexual intercourse may seem impracticable to depraved natures, and yet be perfectly natural and easy to persons properly trained to chastity. Our method simply proposes the subordination of the flesh to the spirit, teaching men to seek principally the elevated spiritual pleasures of sexual connection. This is certainly natural and easy to the spiritual man however difficult it may be to the sensual. In the first place it secures woman from the curses of involuntary and undesirable procreation; and secondly, it stops the drain of life on the part of the man.

The habit of making sexual intercourse a quiet affair, restricting the action of the organs to such limits as are necessary to the avoidance of the crisis, can easily be established, and then there is no risk of conception without intention.

Our theory, separating the amative from the propagative, not only relieves us of involuntary and undesirable procreation, but opens the way to scientific propagation. We believe that propagation, rightly conducted and kept within such limits as life can fairly afford, is a blessing. A very large proportion of all children born under the present system are begotten contrary to the wishes of both parents, and lie nine months in the mother's womb under their mother's curse or a feeling little better than a curse. Such children cannot be well organized. We are opposed to excessive, and consequently, oppressive pro creation, which is almost universal. We are opposed to random procreation, which is unavoidable in the present marriage custom. But we favor an intelligent, well-ordered procreation.

We believe the time will come when involuntary and random propagation will cease, and when scientific combination will be applied to human generation as freely and successfully as it is to that of other animals. And at all events, we believe that good sense and benevolence will very soon sanction and enforce the rule that women shall bear children only when they choose. They have the principal burden of breeding to bear, and they rather than men, should have their choice of time and circumstances.

Strike of a Sex, by George N. Miller, has been read by thousands. (Zugassent's Discovery is the same theory of control as Karezza.) He writes:

To the teachers of the young, Zugassent's Discovery appeals with the voice of a prophet. It concerns the happiness of millions yet to be. If it were taught to the young by enlightened and pure-minded teachers they would never be conscious of any sacrifice. On the contrary, they would prefer it, as has been demonstrated; and the tremendous compensations which such a wise conservation of force would bring would speedily make the earth astir with a new prepotent race.

Those who perceive the crying need for a radical reformation in existing beliefs on sexual subjects, must look to the instruction of the young for the step in advance they earnestly hope to see.

Let the young be taught that it was never nature's intention that man should take pride in his purely animal instincts and desires, and that the progress of the race depends more upon the absolute control of the sexual nature for the improvement of the species than upon any other one thing except the broadest idea of human brotherhood.

Let them be taught that the organs for love's expression are entirely distinct from those of generation, and that it is an unworthy act to use the latter except for nature's purposes; that the proper use of the former raises the sexual act to a mental plane where it ceases to be the brutalizing and degrading animalism it often is, but becomes the next step toward soul development which is the appointed task of man.

And indeed, if a discerning public sentiment could be formed, and the young could be taught by pure-minded teachers, that it would be far better for their own health and happiness, as well as that of their posterity, to regulate their lives by this rule of temperance, a great many happy marriages would be possible which are now cruelly postponed or hopelessly abandoned for fear of the expense and embarrassment of children. It considers the welfare and happiness of others in the most engrossing of human pleasures, and thus partakes of the divine. It lifts the interchanges between the sexes from the purely sensual plane, tending toward death, into that of joyous social and religious fellowship tending toward life. It envelops those who really apprehend it in an atmosphere of purity and chastity sweeter and far more real than that possessed by nuns.

There is today among pure-minded people, who believe that the sexual nature is sacred, holy, and glorious, a crying and insistent demand for a pure and innocent method of limiting the size of their families and mitigating the woes of poverty and ill-health resulting from too frequent child-bearing. Conscientious and God-fearing persons naturally recoil from the methods adopted by the irreligious. They cannot feel that such methods have the justifying and ennobling effect which should pertain to the associations of a sacrament. And shall such people as these be always left to misdirection, chance, and misery? Do not the infinite resources of Christianity contain an assured cure for this evil? Here is one that seems completely to supply this demand. It is not only intrinsically pure and innocent, but in teaching self-control and true temperance, without asceticism, it reacts powerfully for good on the whole character. It is not a merely nugatory device, but a stimulus to spirituality.

The young people who are now approaching marriageable age live in a world whose ideas, in nearly every department of life, have been largely modified, if not completely changed, by the advent of steam, electricity, the microscope, the telescope, the telephone, and other constantly multiplying agents of enlightenment. Is it not reasonable to suppose that there is the same opportunity for infinite improvement and revolutionizing discovery in such a vital department as that of the sex relation, and that the results of such discovery will be commensurate with the immense importance of the subject? The Discovery of Zugassent has been demonstrated to be such an improvement, and it alone provides a sure foundation for the perfect solution both of the sexual and population problems.

The final supremacy over nature lies in the full subjection of man's own body to his intelligent will. There are already an abundance of familiar facts showing the influence of education and direct discipline in developing the powers of the body. We see men every day who, by attention and painstaking investigation and practice in some mechanical art, have gained a power over their muscles, for certain purposes, which to the mere natural man would be impossible or miraculous. In music the great violinists and pianists are examples. All the voluntary faculties are known to come under the power of education, and the human will is found able to express itself in the motions of the body, to an extent and perfection that is in proportion to the pains taking and discipline that are applied. So far as the department of voluntary outward habits is concerned, the influence of will and education to control the body is universally admitted. But there is a step further. Investigation and experience are now ready to demonstrate the power of the will over what have been considered and called the involuntary processes of the body. The mind can take control of them, certainly, to a great extent; the later discoveries point to the conclusion, that there are strictly no involuntary departments in the human system, but that every part falls appropriately and in fact within the dominion of mind, spirit, and will.

As a promoter of domestic happiness and a preventer of the woes that lead to divorce, Zugassent's Discovery is entitled to the lasting gratitude of all good people, as is shown by the many testimonies on record, two of which follow.

Since my husband became acquainted with the philosophy of Zugassent, he has endeared him self to me a hundred-fold, and although our so-called "honeymoon" was passed five years ago, it was no more real, and far less lasting, than the ecstatic, the unspeakable happiness which is now continually mine. My prosaic and sometimes in different husband has changed by a heavenly magic into an ardent and entrancing lover, for whose coming I watch with all the tender raptures of a schoolgirl. His very step sends a thrill through me, for I know that my beloved will grasp me and clasp me and cover me with kisses such as only the most enthusiastic lover could give. And though the years lapse, I cannot see or feel any change in the way he cherishes me. To each other we are continual objects of deepest reverence and the most sacred mystery. Our affection deepens, our romance seems as sure and enduring as the stars. My lover! My hero! My knight! My husband! I date my marriage from the time when he became a disciple of Zugassent, for that was the beginning of our assured happiness.

But it is not alone as a cherishing lover that my husband has become my crown of happiness. He has grown perceptibly nobler in character, in purpose, in strength, in all the qualities that make a man God-like, so that beside a lover I have a strong friend and wise counselor, and my happiness is complete.

L. S. T.

I am a young man, twenty-four years of age, enjoying the most vigorous health. For two years after becoming engaged I delayed marriage, simply because I did not think my income sufficient to support a wife and the children which I regarded as an inevitable consequence. Happily for me a friend, who knew my circumstances, wrote me about Zugassent's Discovery. The ideas contained in this discovery were so different from all my preconceived ideas of what constituted marital happiness, that I was inclined to reject them as utterly impracticable and absurd. But the more I thought of the matter the more clearly I saw that if there was a possibility of these new ideas being true, they were exactly adapted to a man in my circumstances, and that they made my marriage immediately practicable. The wholly new thought that retaining the vital force within himself would naturally make a man stronger, cleaner, and better also seemed to me not irrational. With some misgivings, there fore, I determined to venture upon marriage, and it has been completely successful. I have had a continuous honeymoon for four years. I have never been conscious of any irksome restraint or asceticism in my sexual experience; and my self-control and strength, mental and physical, have greatly increased since my marriage. In the light of my own experience I regard the idea that the seminal fluid is a secretion that must be got rid of as being the most pernicious and fatal one that can possibly be taught to young people.

J. G.

My Dear Dr. Stockham:

Your most gracious answer to my request came promptly. Last evening I devoted to *Karezza* and "Creative Life." I bless you from my heart for this beautiful interpretation of the relation between the sexes. Passion has always seemed to me to be a sharing of God's creative life and a divine instinct. Its perversion and sensuality have profaned the holiest joys, and veiled souls from one another, shutting out the Love which is the very High Priest of the Holy of Holies. All Womankind should give living praise and thanks for the beneficence of Karezza's influence, as I do.

Alice B. Stockham

It is delightful and reassuring to find one's own truest intuitions purely interpreted on an open page. My own nature is filled and vibrant with that creative fire. I have never been ashamed of it, but it has been strongly repressed. I give to my ministry the love-forces that have never been satisfied except by the transfusion of the Universal Love. I believe that the ennoblement of this passion to its own spiritual plane will lift the whole race heavenward, and redeem the home and social world from retrogression. It is the divine regeneration, the new birth of Spiritual Consciousness, for which the world has suffered long and long. Permit me to express my admiration for the dignity, purity and sweet seriousness of style of *Karezza* and the booklets. Accept my very real thanks.

Believe that I shall try to promote, in all ways that a sister minister may, your beneficent message to women.

Yours sincerely, for love and purity,
M.L.L.
Fort Collins, Colo., November 1900.

Dear Dr. Stockham:

My dear wife and I are indeed very grateful for the valuable advice so freely given in your letter and in the books which accompanied it. You will be glad to know that the information enabled us to consummate our marriage in a very beautiful way and we are still lovers, with extended opportunities for showing our affection and devotion for each other. I can truthfully add that the beautiful simile used in your letter of two lives flowing together like waters is applicable to us, and as we think, will be so to the end.

Acting on your advice before marriage, we read together *Karezza* and two of the other books you sent. My dear one was much interested and imbued by your uplifting

84

teaching and the new ideals which it opened up for her. Your excel lent and the most advanced of the other books I thought best that she should read by herself, and she now desires me to ex press to you her heartiest thanks for the former especially, as it gives her just the information she wanted and which she had not been able to obtain elsewhere. She wishes that all these works could be placed in the hands of every prospective bride, as she is quite sure it would save much suffering and misunderstanding at the very beginning of married life.

Yours sincerely, J. A. L.
Birmingham, England, March 28, 1901.

Dear Dr. Stockham:

I want to say that I knew of, believed in, and practiced Karezza long before I knew there was such a book, and still believe it most fully.

The teachings of Karezza came to me in a critical and trying time of my life. I had been married several years, and the harmony between my wife and self seemed dying out. She had loved me dearly, but the old sex embrace had no attraction for her, and grew more and more repulsive. The new teaching brought us into a new heaven and a new earth.

I cannot tell you how happy we became. We were simply lovers, but such lovers as we had never been before. An indescribable tenderness pervaded all our relations. My wife proved a sexual power and perfection rare and wonderful. Her mental and moral nature both developed until I hardly knew her, and I for the first time was sure that I was a poet. And all this ever increased until her death some years after.

Karezza seems to me to be the sex-blending of the moral natures, it seems to call out and arouse to an ecstasy of delight and power the spiritual and poetic nature of both man and woman. It gives strength as if it were the key to unlock powers. Karezza is perfectly successful where the two come together with a mutual loving desire to assist and bless each other, to blend and exchange spiritual gifts, to inspire each other to the noblest moods. Then the "Heaven" stage is easily reached.

J. W. L.

March 1901.

My Dear Dr. Stockham:

A sweet and wise American friend has introduced my dear husband and myself to the pure delights of Karezza, and I should feel myself the basest of ingrates if I left this land without writing you this word of heartfelt thanks; and yet how poor words are to convey real gratitude! We rob words of meaning by our wretched way of using them to express paltry things, and when a benefit has been done one which enriches nay, transforms life the whole world one has but the same old exhausted words.

For this wonderful discovery is in sober reality a transformer of wedded life. I am a woman of passion (until now I have always been ashamed of it). My dear husband is a man of passion; until now it has seemed that it was the one blemish on his noble manhood. How ignorant—nay, how wicked it all seems now.

But, my dear Dr. Stockham, how does it hap pen that the most mighty, the most beautiful of the natural desires that which is at the very foundation of society, and which is connected with all the sanctities of life marriage, with all it ideally means, motherhood fatherhood why is it that this powerful and holy passion has remained under a kind of ban?

Why, we have taken up the latent capacity which is in us for music and have trained and refined it till it ministers now to every highest thing in us, and also affords us the purest pleasure. What a distance from the savage's tom-tom to a modern piano from the discordant savage chant to the intermezzo! We no longer eat with our fingers, tearing half -roasted flesh as we squat about a fire, but have taken up the natural desire for food and made it minister to the sweetest social pleasures. We have put thought and skill and fancy and art to work to lift eating into a great rational pleasure and refinement. And now Karezza has come! How numberless are the benefits! The first and greatest is that, at last, after nine years of legal marriage (and of real love, too), we are really married. There is not a film of constraint, false modesty, or conventionality between us, and with the downfall of the physical barrier has come such a flowing together of soul as I cannot describe. I really have never known my darling until now. He seems to me more beautiful than ever did the Apollo, and so grand and manly in his continence and self-control, while it is perfectly evident that just 7 his nine years wife, and twice a mother am a delight to him, and oh, how satisfying are now the days of happy anticipation and then the happier fulfillment. O dear, joy-giving Dr. Stockham, what satisfaction must be yours as you think how (to thousands, I sup pose), you have brought the purest, truest joys of marriage the real nobility of self-control! Yes, you have brought to light true marriage, and true womanhood as well. I am no longer conscious of being a separate being, ministering to the "animal" desires of my husband as he ministered to mine. "We are taught to dance, to play upon the harpsichord, to embroider, to govern servants, to enter and leave a room properly, but never how to be wives. It is as if we should teach officers how to bow and to dance, but not how to fight. The things worthy of the highest possible development are "left to Nature." Why do we not leave manners and eating and art to Nature?

Those who have an idea of suppressing passion are fatally wrong vain endeavor instead of using and giving it its regnant place. Sir J. and I have had no surer revelation in our hours of spiritual exaltation, through controlled union, than that this passion which God has made strongest and upon which is built the family and social order, is also a nexus of spirit, soul and body. Every power, every emotion, every resource of the volitional life, blend with every thrilling nerve of the physical life in the controlled union.

One of the blissful results of this *vita nuova*, is that we both are perfectly unmoved by others. We are sovereigns in the sphere of our own personal beings. No other crosses the frontier.

Very warmly yours,
Lady J. G. C.

Every person has a right to health, and most especially to that health which gives normal expression of the reproductive functions. Karezza is not an idle theory, as the above testimonials and the experience of many thou sands prove. It is rather a philosophy which is attainable, and which in practice gives most satisfactory results. It is a conscious use of the law of life in regeneration, which not only gives a knowledge of innate powers, and becomes a factor in personal development, but gives a prophecy of progeny that must surpass the most brilliant of all time.

THE KAREZZA METHOD

Preface

It was, I believe, in the winter of 1915–16 that a woman-friend in California wrote and asked me why I did not write a special little book on Karezza.

As events had convinced me that there certainly was crying need of instruction on the matter, her suggestion took root and this small brochure is the fruit.

For though quite a number have written more or less concerning controlled intercourse, they have usually done so guardedly and so vaguely that to the average inquirer the subject remains a mystery and the beginner does not know how to proceed. For which reason most men fail and give up who could just as well succeed. And success or failure here may make all the difference between divorce or a lifetime of love-happiness.

It is my hope that in this work I shall be able to give the world a plain, practical little guidebook to what I consider the most important sexual discovery and practice in all human history.

"Soul Blending"

And still beyond the embrace that begets the body is the embrace that begets the soul, that invokes the soul from the Soul.

The wonderful embraces, sacred, occult and unspeakably tender, pure as prayer;

The hour-long, longer indwelling of him within her, conceiving her again like a child, the hour-long, longer, over-closing of her upon him, bearing him again like a babe in her womb.

The infinite understanding of each by the other, the transcendent uplift of each by the other;

No tumult orgasmal here; not because crushed out, simply because not desired, simply because this is beyond that, a saner, broader joy; the great currents, flowing through wider channels, rage not nor whirl, for where the greater is there the lesser is not demonstrative.

Here is harmony too sweet for violence, osmosis of soul within soul, rhythmically blending, inflowing, outflowing; singing without words; silent music of divine instrument.

Symphony of sex of nerve, heart, thought, and soul in touch, at-one-ing.

Absolute peace, realized heaven, the joy that never disappoints, that exceeds imagination, that cannot be described.

The love ineffable, the inspiration of brain, the energizing of muscle, the illumination of feature, the healing of body, the expression of soul.

Spiritual sex-exchanging; the masculine in her uttering, the feminine in him receiving, positive and negative alternating at will.

Spiritual sex-begetting; the impregnation of each by the other with beautiful thoughts, divine dreams, high hopes, noble ambitions, pure aspirations, clairvoyant vision, the birth-bed of genius.

The giving of each to the other to the uttermost impulse of blessing, the receiving of each by the other to the uttermost nerve terminal of body, to the uttermost fine filament of spirit.

Not followed by exhaustion, but by days of genius, clear and exalted vision, buoyant and happy health.

Not followed by revulsion, but by hours, days, weeks, years, a lifetime, maybe, of tender memories, clinging, affectionate longing to caress again, to be re-embracing.

(Nay, is it not true, beyond all truth, that those who have once thus bathed, blended, soul in soul, are eternally married?)

The embrace of at-one-ness, of expression, and purification and revivification, that incarnates the divine in the human.

Not possible except to the pure and poetic, to true and innocent lovers, fitting, responding, liberating.

To whom soul and body are both sacred, to whom this communion is a religious rite the most sacred.

The embrace of the Cosmic souls, the angel-mates in their heaven.

No vision this, dear friends, no poetic metaphor merely, for lo! I have lived it all many, many times, hundreds of others have lived it many times, every member of the race shall sometime, in some life, live it.

It is joy and truth, the joy of joys and truth of truths.
KAREZZA.

CHAPTER 1

What Is Karezza?

Karezza is controlled, non-seminal intercourse. The word Karezza (pronounced "ka-ret-za") is from the Italian and means a caress. Alice B. Stockham, M.D., was the first one who applied it as the distinctive name of the art and method of sexual relations without orgasmal conclusion. But the art and method itself was discovered in 1844 by John Humphrey Noyes, the founder of the Oneida Community, by experiences and experiments in his own marital life. He called it "Male Continence." Afterwards George N. Miller, a member of the Community, gave it the name of "Zugassent's Discovery" in a work of fiction, *The Strike of a Sex*.

There are objections to both these names. Zugassent was not a real person and therefore did not discover it. It was Noyes' Discovery, in fact. Continence, as Dr. Stockham points out, has come to mean abstinence from all intercourse. The Oneida Communists do not appear to have opposed the female orgasm, and therefore it was well enough for them to name it "Male Continence," but Dr. Stockham and I agree that in the highest form and best expression of the art neither man nor, woman has or desires to have the orgasm, and therefore it is no more male than female continence. And a single-word name is always more convenient than a compound. For which reasons I have accepted Dr. Stockham's musical term, which is besides, beautifully suggestive and descriptive. Another writer on this art (I first heard of it through him; he deriving it from Noyes) was Albert Chavannes, who in a little book on it, called it *Magnetation*, a name which I coined for him. It is perhaps not a bad name; but I now think "Karezza" better.

Noyes' honor to the discovery has been disputed. Others, it is asserted, discovered it before him or independently since.

(Since writing the above I have become acquainted with a Dr. E. Elmer Keeler, of Syracuse, New York, who tells me that he made the independent discovery of Karezza, by his own sex-experiences in early manhood, and for years taught it in private lectures, both to the laity and the profession, before he learned of Noyes and his teaching—a sufficient commentary, if any were needed, on the ignorance not only of the general public but even of the doctors on this most important matter. Not knowing of any other, Keeler gave it the name of "Sex-Communion," but defining the term as "*all* forms of sexual expression in which no emission occur," thus still leaving a need for a specific term to name the definite internal act, which Karezza as a term does.)

Various Europeans and Asiatics probably discovered America before Columbus, but he first made it known and helpful to the world at large, and therefore the honor is rightfully his. Exactly so with Noyes—he first made Karezza available to mankind in general.

His little work "Male Continence" is a model of good argument on the matter; but I believe *Karezza*, by Dr. Stockham, is the only book now in print which treats of it. Several other small works have appeared, but mostly they treat of the subject in such poetic and transcendental terms that the seeker after practical instruction is left still seeking.

All writers, too, have tacitly assumed that the woman could do as she pleased in the matter and that success or failure all depended on the man. I regard this as a fundamental error and the cause of most disappointments. Considerations such as these have mainly decided me to write this little work. At this time of agitation on birth control, also, it appears timely. And beyond all looms the extraordinary, one might say unaccountable ignorance of it, not only of ordinary sexual students, but of practically all physicians and even the greatest sexual specialists and teachers.

Actually, the general public knows more about it than its educators. Thus Forel, in his *Sexual Question*, never mentions it at all, and therefore presumably never heard of it. Bloch, in his professedly exhaustive work *The Sexual Life of Our Times*, though he once mentions Dr. Stockham on another matter, has only one ambiguous paragraph in the whole book that can possibly refer to Karezza (apparently some imperfect form of it), disapproving of it on theory only, evidently, without the slightest personal knowledge, or even observation. Havelock Ellis, in the *Psychology of Sex*, is more instructed and favorable, but appears to have derived his knowledge almost entirely from the Oneida Communists; not at all at first hand. And the general ignorance, indifference, or aversion, even to any experiment, among men, is simply amazing. Most men say at once that it is impossible, most physicians that it is injurious, though with no kind of real knowledge. Most women, on the other hand, who have had any experience of it, eulogize it in unmeasured terms, as the very salvation of their sexual life, the very art and poetry of love, which indeed it is, but, as most men will not attempt it, most women are necessarily kept in ignorance of its inestimable benefits to their sex.

The first objection that is certain to meet one who would recommend Karezza is that it is "unnatural." Noyes confronts this objection very ably, and it is indeed absurd, when you came to think of it, to hear men who drink alcohol, smoke, use tea and coffee, take milk though adults, eat cooked food, live in heated houses, wear clothes, write books, shave their faces, use machinery, and do a thousand and one things which the natural man, the true aborigine, knew nothing of, condemn a mere act of moderation and self-control in pleasure as "unnatural."

They do not stop to think that, if their appeal is to original or animal nature, then they must never have intercourse with the female at all, except when she invites it, is in a certain condition, at certain seasons of the year, and for procreation only. For all intercourse as a love act is clearly "unnatural" in their use of the term. How would they relish that?

These same men will recommend and have their women use douches, drugs, and all sorts of mechanical means to nullify the natural consequences of their act, with never a lisp of protest at the unnaturalness of it all.

As a matter of fact, Karezza is absolutely natural. It employs Nature only and from first to last. To check any act which prudence suggests, or experience has shown, likely to have undesired consequences, is something constantly done throughout all Nature, even among the lowest animals. Karezza is such a check. It is simply prudence and skill in the sexual realm, changing its form and direction of activity in such wise that the desired pleasure may be more fully realized and the undesired results avoided—nothing more.

The denunciation of it as injurious is almost equally an expression of thoughtless prejudice. I have now had personal knowledge of it for over forty years. I learned of it from A. Chavannes, who with his wife had practiced it twenty years. It has been before the American people since 1846. The Oneida Communists practiced it, Havelock Ellis states, thirty years.

I have known members of the Oneida Community. I have read all I possibly could on it, talked with everyone I could hear of who had knowledge of it; I have yet to meet or hear of a single woman who has the slightest accusation to make against it on the score of injury to health or disagreeable sensations or after effects. Three only (all with slight experience) told me they thought there was more pleasure in the old embrace; the others most emphatically to the contrary.

Van de Warker, says, Havelock Ellis, "studied forty-two women of the community, without finding any undue prevalence of reproductive diseases, nor could he find any diseased condition attributable to the sexual habits of the community." Contrast this with the usual sex-relation, which is constantly being accused, particularly by women, of causing all sorts of injurious and painful consequences, apparently upon the best of evidence.

After twenty-five years experience, the Oneida Community, upon request of the New York Medical Gazette, instituted "a professional examination" and had a report made by Theodore R. Noyes, M.D., in which it was shown, by careful comparison of our statistics with those of the U. S. census and other public documents, that the rate of nervous diseases in the Community is considerably below the average of ordinary society. This report was published by the *Medical Gazette* and was pronounced by the editor "a model of careful observation; bearing intrinsic evidence of entire honesty and impartiality."

Physicians freely condemn it or express doubts of it almost invariably with no knowledge of it of any kind. They think it should cause ill-health, and therefore they say it will. It is said to cause nervousness, prostatitis, an inflamed state of organs, etc.

Now we all know how much pure guesswork figures in so-called medical "science"; how often that which merely coincides is asserted to hold a relation of cause and effect. However I think I can see how, very easily, the ignorant or imperfect use of this art might lead to the above-described bad results.

In ideal and successful Karezza, the sexual passion is transmuted and sublimated, to a greater or less degree, into tenderness and love, and the thought is maintained that the orgasm is not desired or desirable. Now if a man, on the contrary, entered the embrace with the thought that he terribly desired the orgasm, but by the sheer force of will must prevent it; if he excited himself and his partner to the utmost sexual furore, but at last denied it culmination; caring nothing for love at any time, but for sex only all the time, I can see how, very reasonably, his denied passion might react disastrously on his nervous system, just as any strongly repressed emotion may. Just as a man who indulges in the most furious thoughts of rage, but clenches his fists and shuts his mouth tight, rather than express it, may burst a blood vessel or get an apoplexy. This may indeed be a sort of "male continence," on the physical side, but real Karezza, as I know it and would present it, is very different.

Real Karezza requires preparatory mental exercise. It requires first the understanding and conviction that the spiritual, the caressive, the tender side of the relation is much more important, much more productive of pleasure in fact, than the merely sexual, and that throughout the whole relation the sexual is to be held subordinate to this love side as its tool, its agent, its feeder. Sex is indeed required to furnish all it has to the feast, but strictly under the leadership of and to the glory of love.

It requires, second, the understanding and profound conviction that in this kind of love-feast the orgasm is a marplot, a killjoy, an awkward and clumsy accident, and the end of everything for the time, therefore most undesired.

It requires, third, an understanding of the psychological law that all emotions are to a considerable extent capable of being "sublimated," that is expressed in a different direction and with reference to another object than that first intended.

We have all seen orators or actors first arouse an audience to emotional intensity and then direct that emotion at pleasure to laughter or tears, to love or hate, revenge or pity, lust or purity. Taking full advantage of this law, the Karezza artist sublimates a portion of his sexual passion into the more refined, intellectual, poetic and heart-sweet expression of feeling, thus preventing it from ever reaching that pitch of local intensity which demands explosive discharge. In other words the soul, taking over the blind sex-emotion, diffuses it and irradiates the whole being for a prolonged period with its joy-giving, exalting potency. This might be compared to a man who had a barrel of gunpowder where with to celebrate, whereupon instead of firing the entire cask in one mighty explosion (orgasm) he made it into fireworks for the esthetic enjoyment of a whole evening. Observe that, either way, all the powder would be burned, only in the second form the display covers a much greater length of time, is more refined, artistic, and complexly satisfying.

Such is Karezza to the orgasm. It is art, intellect, morality, and estheticism in sexual enjoyment instead of crude, reckless appetite.

Still this comparison does not do Karezza justice. When the powder is burned, it is gone, but it is not at all so with Karezza. In Nature, something accumulates in the organism for the endowment of the offspring. Much of man's food consists of what lower forms of life have stored up for their children. We largely live on starch, honey, gluten, seeds, milk, eggs, robbed from babies that were to be. In our own bodies, also, we store up a reproductive surplus to be given to our progeny. This is probably not simply one thing, but many things—love, magnetism, vital force, seed, perhaps other things that we know nothing about today. And indeed we do not know very accurately about any of these things today, but we do know that something is stored up in us, and that its presence in us makes us vivid, brilliant, beautiful, powerful, like a stimulating food. It is a life-food or life-force, intended to be given to our children, but we also can feed on it or give it to each other.

Love between a man and woman seems to be such a process of mutually exchanging and feeding on this surplus life-force. When they enter each other's aura, there is an interchange of male and female food-values; the nearer they are to each other the stronger and more satisfying the exchange, and their "love" to each other is the craving for such an exchange or the thing itself, hence the craving for closeness and touch.

In Karezza, both by reason of its intense intimacy and of the long time of contact, besides the peculiar fitness of the organs themselves for the work, this exchange reaches its maximum of realization. It is vital exchange in its most satisfying expression, wherefore it is really the thing for which all love is reaching, wishing.

Apparently, in the love-contact of two, some of this life-food is released in each and reabsorbed in each, but more of it is given to the other partner. Men and women in love are thus veritable cannibals and feed each on each, and each gives to the other the stored-up life-food, charged with the personal qualities of maleness or femaleness of the individual sex. Apparently my lover and I may live on our life-foods to some extent, but each finds the life-food of the other the more stimulating and nutritious. In Karezza, we feed each other "baby food."

Explain the process as we may, this fact is sure: that in successful Karezza, the sex-organs become quiet, satisfied, demagnetized as perfectly as by the orgasm, while the rest of the body of each partner glows with a wonderful vigor and conscious joy, or else with a deep, sweet, contentment, as after a happy play; tending to irradiate the whole being with romantic love; and always with an after-feeling of health, purity and wellbeing.

We are most happy and good-humored as after a full meal. Whereas, if there has been an orgasm, it is the common experience that there is a sense of loss, weakness, and dispelled illusion; following quickly on the first grateful feeling of relief. There has been a momentary joy, but too brief and epileptic to make much impression on consciousness, and now it is gone, leaving no memory. The lights have gone out, the music has stopped. The weakness is often so severe as to cause pallor, faintness, vertigo, dyspepsia, disgust, irritability, shame, dislike, or other pathological or unloving symptoms. This especially on the man's part, but perhaps to some extent on the woman's part too. Even if no more, there is lassitude, sudden indifference, a wish to sleep. A wet blanket has fallen for the time at least, on the flame of love. Romance drops and crawls like a winged bird.

In Karezza, on the contrary, the partners unfold and separate reluctantly, lingeringly, kissing, clinging, petting to the last, thrilled with and rehearsing memories, glowing with an affection and admiration which they feel can never end.

It would appear that in the orgasmal embrace the life-force is thrown off with such suddenness and volume that it is quite impossible for the partner to receive or assimilate much of it, therefore most of it is utterly wasted.

For this reason, the orgasmal-embrace is a most clumsy and disappointing thing when employed as a love-embrace. Nature meant it only for propagation, and its whole modus operandi is calculated to check love, defeat love, and turn love into indifference or aversion. The more frequently it is employed, the more love dies, romance evaporates, and a mere sexuality, a matter-of-fact relation, or plain dislike, takes the place of the glamour of courtship days. On the contrary, Karezza makes marriage more delicious than courtship, more romantic than wooing, and maintains an endless, satisfying honeymoon.

There is an increase of attractiveness and magnetism of each for each, a growth of satisfaction in each other's society, affection, and caressing becomes a sweet habit. Nothing else known makes the course of true love run so smooth as Karezza.

The orgasm is not always, but very commonly, followed by a greater or less degree of exhaustion, perhaps extreme. But Karezza, unless repeated to excess or practiced between the mismated, is never followed by exhaustion but often by a delightful glow and joy in life. The usual sequel to the orgasm is demagnetization, indifference, too frequently irritability, disgust, repulsion and a craving for stimulants, but Karezza irradiates the whole being with tender, romantic, peaceful love.

This, so far as I know, is universal experience, and therefore merely needs to be stated to show how healthful an influence Karezza must wield. As a matter of fact, because of the tonicity, glow and vigor it bestows on the sexual parts and its wine-like inspiration of the spirit of the partners, with no reaction, it is one of the best hygienic agencies for the benefit and cure of ordinary sexual weaknesses and ailments—leucorrhea, displacements, prolapsus, bladder-troubles, simple urethritis, prostatitis, etc.—known. And I say this from actual knowledge. I have known it to act like magic in painful menstruation and in prostatitis.

But remember, I am always speaking of its exercise between those who are naturally fitted to respond and who really love each other, who honor their bodies and would not knowingly abuse them. As a mere sex-experiment, it might be of little value or satisfaction. It appears to be perfect or poor, just about in proportion to the greater or less amount of heart-love involved. At least it imperatively demands kindness, tenderness, chivalry on the man's part, a pleased acceptance and relaxation on the woman's; and the more refinement, poetry of feeling and mutual romance the better. Any amount can be utilized. The gross, reckless and lustful may as well let it alone—it is not for them.

As a nerve sedative its effect is remarkable. I have known it to instantly cure a violent, even agonizing nervous headache, a restful nap following upon the cessation of pain. Under a strong, gentle magnetic man, a nervous woman often falls into a baby-like sleep, in the very midst of the embrace, and this is felt to be a peculiar luxury and coveted experience. Many women call Karezza "The Peace." Others call it "Heaven." This alone is a testimony worth volumes.

S. G. Lewis, of Grass Valley, California, in his *Hints and Keys to Conjugal Felicity*, is especially rich in testimony to the spiritual and romantic value of Karezza, but his fine little work is long out of print.

Now I do not apprehend from all I have seen of life that Karezza will ever come into vogue from the male side of the world. Men seem united in their dull, lethargic indifference to it. Helplessly or selfishly, they say it is impossible and let it go at that, rather than make the little effort required to perfect themselves in it. They would preferably choose, or rather oblige their women to choose, something out of the nerve-shocking, disgusting, disease-producing outfit of douches, drugs, tampons, plugs, pessaries, shields, condoms, and save them all further responsibility in the matter, although the highest authorities admit none of these resources are really safe—that is, sure—contraceptives, and most of them are decidedly injurious.

Only the absence of semen is safe, and that is found in Karezza and in Karezza alone. But perhaps the most clinching condemnation of these methods, to a refined person, is that pronounced by a fine woman of my acquaintance: "There is not one of these methods that does not destroy, for the woman, all the poetry of the act." Only in Karezza is the poetry fully preserved, and not only that, but made capable of development to the most refined nuances of artistic and ingenious delight. Only to the Karezza-lover is the Art of Love possible in any sense worthy of the name. All the others begin the performance by shutting off the music and throwing away the wine.

But as the Woman Movement grows, I am sure Karezza will come into its own. As women learn its transcendent importance to their happiness and health, they will demand it and refuse all men that cannot supply that demand. That will be a force that cannot be withstood.

Woman is by birth the Queen of Love and will certainly assume her inheritance and control in her own sphere and realm.

CHAPTER 2

Magnetation

As I have said, I coined for Albert Chavannes, as a title for his little brochure on this subject, the word "Magnetation." This was intended to express the theory, then so prevalent, that the thrills and pleasures of sex and love were caused by the transmission and reception of currents of "animal magnetism" or "vital electricity," which could be conveyed by contact or passes from one human body to another, and that diseases even could be cured by the same agency, as in "laying on of hands."

There has been much controversy on this matter. It has been argued by some that the "currents," the "magnetic attractions," etc., felt by the susceptible, were purely imaginary and ideological—that the lover induced his own thrills, the patient cured himself. We may waive much of this. While today one hears very little of this magnetism, the fact remains that the presence and the touch, explain it as we may, of certain people give us intense, vivid feelings and produce powerful reactions, while the presence and touch of others may shock, or leave us indifferent or repelled. Practically this is sufficient. This seems like magnetic action, and for all our purposes we may assume that the seeming is a fact.

It is assumed, therefore, that ordinarily the male is positive to the female, who is negative to him, and the masculine organs are positive to the feminine organs. This may be called the normal or usual relation, but it is possible to voluntarily or involuntarily reverse this, and in most cases, between lovers in close contact, certain parts in each are negative to the contacting parts of the other, which may be positive to them.

This fact—that the entire personality, in all its parts, is not necessarily positive or negative at the same time—is one important to remember, for it explains much and is like a key to the whole art of Karezza. Thus a woman may be very positive and even dominant in her love, while her body remains most alluringly passive. Or she may open her eyes and make them positive, while the rest remains negative. Or she may put positiveness into the caress of her hands alone, or will it into some other part of her being, or entirely assume and play the masculine, positive part, while the man assumes the feminine. Of this, more will be said later.

But in general, though the woman allures and makes herself a drawing lodestone, it is the man who takes and should take the active, positive role and is "the artist in touch." The man who would succeed in Karezza, then, must cultivate the art of magnetic touch. He should learn to think of himself as an electric battery, of which it may be said that the right hand is the positive pole (in right-handed people only, of course), and the left hand the negative, capable of transmitting to other and receptive human beings an electric current. If both his hands are in contact with someone, he must feel the current flowing from his right hand through the body he touches into his left hand, and he must learn how to reverse this and send a current at will from his left hand to his right hand. If he touches with only one hand, or one part, then he must feel that he touches positively and the flesh he touches is negative or receptive to him. He must learn to will the current he gives through the body he touches, through its nerves, to any part he wishes to electrify, to thrill, or to soothe, and to feel convincingly that he is doing so. In Karezza his organs must ordinarily be felt to be positive and the woman's negative, for the best results to both. He may even practice on himself, learning to feel his own magnetism, to test it; and how to cure various pains and ailments by his own touch.

Understand me—a man may succeed beautifully in Karezza who has done nothing of all this, nor even heard of it, because of natural magnetism and intuition of what to do, but even he would do better to consciously understand his powers and deliberately will to direct their use.

The fact that magnetic touch has been found a successful method of invigorating the weak and curing the sick, is one proof that should never be overlooked that Karezza, practiced normally, with a wise avoidance of excess, is not only not injurious, as so often claimed, but is really conducive to health. I have been told that Harry Gaze, the Western lecturer, advocates Karezza as a means of maintaining eternal youth, and personally I am convinced that nothing else known is so efficient in preserving youth, hope, beauty, romance, and the joy of life.

A man should learn, therefore, to touch the woman he loves in such a way that he transmits to her a vivid electric current that thrills her with delightful feeling, while it relieves his nervous tension of accumulated surplus force. At the same time, if the parties are well-mated, she will be generating and returning, in some roundabout way, something to him, which equally satisfies him, prevents all sense of loss, and makes him equally thrilled and happy. There is a circuit and exchange which finally perfectly balances and leaves each content.

The man who would be an artist in touch must learn to put this vital elixir into his fingertips, his palms, into the glance of his eyes, suggest it in the tones of his voice, convey it at will from any part of his body which may touch the body of another—yes, even to convey it by mere aura, invisibly, secretly, to another body, near, but not in contact. He must learn to touch with firm and thrilling strength, or with tender gentleness and restfulness. He must learn to stroke and caress with an exquisite delicacy, tactfulness and grace, suggesting music. In the actual embrace he must learn to alternate violent speed and force (yet controlled and never really rude or inconsiderate), in his movements, with touches delicate and soothing, in a contrast of symphonic "storm and peace," which may sink to absolute quietude of strong, tender enfolding.

Oh, touch me, touch me right! she said —
(O God, how often womanhood hath said!)
That we two ones as one be wed,
That all with all, throughout, we wed,
Close, close and tender close! she said,
The touch that knows, O Man! she said
O touch me, touch me right! she said.

The ideal of the woman should be to apprehend with exquisite intuition every mood of the man almost before he knows it himself and to meet it with sympathy, comprehension and response—relaxing, revivifying, restraining, applauding, reinforcing, encouraging, quieting, or thrilling as his need may be. She must realize that her love and admiration are really the psychic basis of the whole relation. The ideal of the man must be to manifest a glorious strength, and passion, held, as a rider would hold a mettled stallion, under an equally glorious control—to prove himself as skillful and chivalrous as heroic. Thus each will be irradiated by the glowing admiration of the other, which is the highest bliss of love.

Probably the most untellably delightful of all human sensations is to touch the flesh of a perfectly mated lover, where the soul is innocent, the heart satisfied, and the magnetic currents seem divinely strong.

There is so much, so much,
In human touch!

CHAPTER 3

Cleanness

Always in the sexual life there should be cleanness—that innocence, kindness, justice of feeling which instinctively prefers any sacrifice of immediate passional pleasure rather than befoul or degrade a high ideal, or to jeopardize the physical or spiritual health of the beloved, or of self, or of the tenderly considered, possible unborn.

Cleanness expresses itself in a reverent regard and considerate self-control at all times, concerning all things, thoughts, motions, and relations of sex, and the conscientious use of all organs and functions in the service of the soul's ideal.

The clean may be mistaken, but whatever they do, they cannot be impure.

CHAPTER 4

Sex and Soul

Sex is very close to soul. Whoso touches sex touches the secrets and centers of life. This is the Mid-Spot, the Origin, the Crux, the Mystery. In sex, the soul is naked. At the contacts of sex the soul trembles, quivers, is shaken to its midmost. The voice of sex, in its power, is as the voice of God—the most imperious and certain-to-be-obeyed call known in Nature or to man.

Sex, soul, religion, and morality are not to be separated. They belong together. The first reverence we detect in Nature is that of the male for the female, of offspring for mother. There is fear elsewhere, but here are mysterious adumbrations and blendings of attraction, adoration, worshipful obedience and withdrawing respect. Sex-religion was the first religion of man, and we shall never get back again to true religion until we again see God in his creative motions, and worship and reverence the soul in flesh.

Sincerity, seriousness, cleanness, generosity, and liberty in sex are the foundations of morality. Where these are found, we have genuine love, true relations, open souls, fearless hearts, fragrant bodies, healthy children, happy mothers, a society everywhere honest, free, and kind. Where these or any of them are lacking, society rots, lies fester, men exist by crime, and shame broods like a cloud.

J. William Lloyd

The agitation of the youth who blushes, trembles, and stammers before the woman he loves; of the girl who melts in his arms, not daring to lift her eyes, dumb, soul-shaken, overcome by the mystery of her being and emotions—these reveal by signs ineffable the sacred seriousness of sex.

CHAPTER 5

When Sex Satisfies

For all finer natures, sex relations are only satisfying when touched by moral and religious emotion—when they are serious, when they involve the depths, when they inspire to the heights.

When sex feels sacred in the use, it gives a divine innocence to the moment, a satisfying sweetness of recollection in the memory.

Sex is only satisfying where it is absolutely free, in a liberty made new and genuine by glad, mutual consent at every moment of its being.

Sex only satisfies when on both sides there are kindness, innocence, consideration—a love that is goodness in expression; that gives and blesses.

Sex only satisfies the finer natures when it unites souls, not merely copulates bodies for a thrill.

An atmosphere of frivolity, recklessness, mere hedonism and indulgence about sex, invariably reacts in disgust—the conscience instantly stamps this as "sin."

Sex having two offices—to unite souls and propagate bodies—there are for these offices two unions: Karezza-union for the deeper love; orgasmal-union for physical begetting. Do not make the mistake of using the latter for the former.

But sex is also like a food, and sexual contact with vital magnetic exchange at certain not-too-long intervals, varying with different temperaments, conditions, and times of life, seems necessary for health and satisfying living, and is also a perfectly valid and justifying reason for sexual embraces and caresses, even where there is only innocent need on one side and tender kindness on the other, or where on both sides there is only need and kindness. There is biological reason to suppose that the function of sex to mysteriously feed and rejuvenate is its oldest and perhaps most essential function, antedating its reproductive function a long, long time.

Starting then from the beginning, the functions of sex may be read as three:

First: to feed and rejuvenate by contact-pressure (perhaps by a sort of catalysis) and a mysterious generation, interchange and mutual exchange of subtle processes and forces.

Second: physical reproduction—child-creation.

Third: soul-union, the mystery of love, affection, spiritual-companionship, mental-inspiration. In all its normal aspects sex is creative and uniting, kind and life-giving in function.

CHAPTER 6

Duality and Spirituality in Sex

Unless we recognize that sex is spiritual as well as physical, we shall not understand how it is the great agent of love. For love is the uniting principle in the universe, and as all things have their opposites, that which reconciles and at-ones them, marries them, is that which we term sex. In the physical organs of male and female, sex is objectified in fixed forms, but this in only one example, and a very small one, of sex. These organs relate peculiarly to physical union and reproduction, but when we come to consider all the various ways in which sex unites and reproduces we find no limitations to these tools. On the contrary, the "duality" which philosophers constantly recognize in Nature is nothing but the larger sex-relation and interaction. All chemical attractions and repulsions, all electrical, are sexual. But we shall not understand this at all if we think always of men and women as such, or of physical males and females when we say sex.

Physical sex-forms are often very deceptive. Some women are more masculine than the average man, and vice versa, which accounts for much of the phenomena of homosexuality. In all deep-seated friendships between those of the same external sex, it will be observed that spiritually one represents the masculine element, one the feminine. And masculine women normally love and marry feminine men. And when such come together, while his physical sex is male and hers female, so that physically he may impregnate her, she is spiritually male and may spiritually impregnate him and beget spiritual children in his brain and soul (that is, thoughts, ideals, purposes, emotions) that change and rule his whole character.

But the complexity by no means stops here. Each person is dual in sex, both in body and in each organ and part. We still remember our divine ancestry, still are androgyne and hermaphrodite. And this is not only so, but it is variably, changeably so. Sex alternates and plays through us all the time, partly involuntarily, partly as we will it. It varies even with difference in weather, food, fatigue, health, and all external impressions and internal evolutions. Thus one listening to an argument may be altogether negative, receptive, feminine in mind, till some word or thought changes the mood, and then, instantly, positive, projective, masculine. This change of mental sex possible, in the same person of either physical sex, within a few moments of time.

This has a very practical relation to Karezza. In its long, blending, intimate embrace of body and soul, a great deal more than the more obvious sex-organs and functions are concerned. A similar sexual interchange takes place between all corresponding parts of body and mind, every function and every thought. Thus while her pelvis may be feminine to his, her bosom may be masculine to his breast; his hands may be more masculine than hers, but her mouth and tongue more positive than his. His intellect may be dominatingly masculine to her mind, and yet in emotion and feeling she may control. And this may at any moment be all reversed. And this may be true not only of regions, but of small parts of regions, single muscles or nerves in one being masculine or feminine, according to health or stimulus, without regard to the possibly opposite condition of the surrounding parts. So of every thought, emotion or word. Could anyone view the two lovers physically, I fancy he would see streams of sex-force flowing from each to the other from every part, eagerly received, drunk up and returned, till it would be hard to tell which one was the most masculine or feminine. If the streams of magnetism were objectified to the eye, they would appear like filaments, making the two forms appear to be literally sewn and tied, netted and interwoven together by innumerable millions of little threads of electrical love and commerce. No wonder love is called "attachment."

But more than this, an unconscious change of mood or thought, or a conscious effort of the will can reverse the sex of any part and make that instantly feminine which before was masculine, or turn feminine to masculine. This may be done skillfully and with delightful effect by those trained in sex-expression. The sexual motions and magnetisms, the touch of the skin, of the hands, the glance of the eyes, the kiss of the lips, the tones of the voice, all these can be instantly reversed from a tender, yielding, clinging, drawing, appealing receptiveness to a bold, positive, thrilling bestowal of vital force. It is plain, then, that the more points on which two lovers are unlike, yet capable of easy and loving exchange, the greater their capacity to give each other joy.

Those who aspire to sexual genius and mastership should take deep note of this, for it is very important. One's power to give sexual joy and satisfaction depends upon one's power to give one's partner a cup for every stream and a drink for every thirst—in other words, to give sex-force where the partner's desire is to receive, and to receive

119

sex-force where the partner desires to give. All this can be learned and acquired, just as other controls and other self-directions can be acquired. It is simply tact and adaptation in the realm of sex. The woman who can be sweet, yielding, tender, receptive to the man when he is sexually virile and strong, and motherly, helpful, executive, when he is dispirited and weak, has vastly more sexual charm than one who can only be timid and passive, or who is always assertive and manlike. And the more easily and skillfully these changes can be made in the same embrace, to meet differing moods, exercise different desires, and to prevent monotony, the longer the embrace can continue, the greater its benefits and joy.

Karezza is exactly like music—it may be only a rude monotonous rhythm, or mere chant or refrain, or it can attain any perfection of harmonic or symphonic complexity and execution. The character and individuality of the players, their natural genius or "ear" for the changes, and their acquired experience and skill being the determining factors, together with the quality and "tune" of the instruments themselves.

Genius in sexual expression is just as normal and certain of occurrence as any other, and some day artists in love will be known and recognized as such—nay, even today, under all our incubus of repression and Grundyism, they are known and admired.

And it will be recognized that the sexual organism, strung with its vibrating and, delicate nerves, is an instrument more perfect than any violin or harp, capable of as exquisite harmonies under the touch of a master. Yet, even as the perfect music is not that which the mere perfection of technique produces, but that into which the true artist breathes his passion and his life, so it is with sex.

It is not simply the man of training, the one who knows how, but the man who loves his instrument, and throws the passion and enthusiasm of his soul into the expression, who elicits the divine melody.

All art demands the lover, and sex-art is the art of the lover.

CHAPTER 7

Sex-Commerce and the Elixir of Life

I believe that sex runs through all life, animal and vegetable—perhaps through the inorganic world also—and that the sexes are cannibals, feeding on each other. The sexes are food to each other.

I believe that both sexes are in the simplest unicellular organism. That afterwards, as life evolves, there is a tendency to a division of labor—to separate the sexes into two persons, but that always the two sexes are more or less in one. Always the male is part female, the female part male, in varying degrees of more or less.

I believe that the processes of life require as an essential a frequent, if not constant, interchange of maleness with femaleness. I believe this takes place within the organism constantly and in proportion to its perfection there is beauty and health. In every cell there is this interchange, and between different cells of the organism there is such an exchange.

But just as in-and-in breeding finally "runs out" the strain and leads to deterioration, so in-and-in exchange of maleness and femaleness—really the same thing—leads to deterioration at last, though many things may assist to delay and postpone the process: change in nourishment, in environment, etc.

Therefore the maleness of one person needs exchange with the femaleness of some other person; the femaleness of one with the maleness of another.

Homosexuality bases partly on the fact that this exchange may be effected, with more or less satisfaction, sometimes, with persons of the same sex (who, as both sexes are in one, are more or less persons of the opposite sex also) but this too is a form of in-and-in exchange, therefore the normal and best exchange is with persons whose sex is visibly and predominantly opposite to one's own. Man normally goes to woman, woman to man. And even here very opposite temperaments are usually preferred, the smooth by the hairy, the red-headed by the black-haired, the fat, by the lean, etc., because these have existed under very different environments, have fed on different nourishment, which they exchange through sex, and, so still further put away in-and-in exchange and complement each other's lacks—Nature always seeking an equilibrium and redistribution of elements in alternation.

This exchange and mutual feeding can be effected in any way in which the sexes can come into each other's aura, but it is most easily effected by touch, and most perfectly by the complete union of Karezza. The sexual orgasm, having an entirely different purpose—that is, not the nourishment of the two individuals concerned, but the transmission of life and nourishment to another, a new and third organism starting from these two—tends rather to defeat and prevent the nourishment of the two and is normally limited, usually, to propagation. To indulge in the orgasm frequently, as a mere pleasure and indulgence, is to create a vice: salacity.

I do not pretend to know what this sexual food is. We may theorize that it is a "flux of electrons," a "current of corpuscles," "hormones," or what not—who knows?—but its effects we may see. The thrill, the vigor, the brilliancy, the glow of lovers; the "illusion," the "glamour," the "romance" of love, we all know. This means swift exchange and joyous feasting. Suppose we call this food the Elixir of Life?

But the mere suggestion of this sexual exchange seems to marvelously quicken and benefit even the inward in-and-in exchanges. Thus reading a love letter or a love story, handling a keepsake, thinking of a lover, and a thousand other such things may benefit the whole being by sex suggestion.

There are those who claim that the cells of the animal organism go to seed and that each one of these little molecules, or corpuscles, go to the ova or spermatozoa to represent that cell in the new organism to be formed by reproduction, so that the essence of everything in the parent organism may be in the offspring. And there are Karezza-ites who explain the thrill and exhilaration of Karezza by claiming that during its exercise these vital seed-elements, not being thrown off by an orgasm, are thrown instead into the circulation again and become a nerve food and cell-elixir; perhaps leading to the return to the germ or sperm of new seed-elements more vivified and electric than before. And that this explains why the mere autosuggestion of love, above alluded to, if intense enough, by somewhat the same process, seems to vitalize like Karezza.

This may not ultimately prove scientific, but I am inclined to accept it and reconcile it with the preceding—to believe that love is a process of self-feeding and redistribution of elements within the organism as well as of mutual feeding and exchange between lovers.

And I believe that all human love that naturally seeks expression in embracing is, at least largely, moved by and based upon this human need of vital exchange and sexual rejuvenation.

Moreover, morally, we need to recognize that this desire of the sexes for hugging, kissing, caressing, contact, closeness, and the most pressing and intimate touch is not vicious or suspicious, but a physiological, a food desire. One needs meats of sexual touch just as one needs meals of food, only not so often. The fullest life cannot be lived without them. However, there can be sexual gluttony, just as there can be food gluttony. And there can be foul, poisonous, unhealthy sexual touches and contacts, just as there can be poisonous, foul, unhealthy viands. Intelligence, selection, self-control, refinement, hygienic wisdom and education, and a sensitive conscience, are needed with both. But neither should be regarded from the attitude of prejudice or mere sentiment, or convention, but from that of science, common sense and the ideal.

CHAPTER 8

The Wine of Sex

The sexual elixir, essence, magnetism—whatever it is in the human blood—is the true natural stimulant and joy-giver of life. It is this that gives the "illusion," the "glamour," the romance," the "blindness," the "madness," the "thrill," and all the rest of which the lore of love tells us. All other stimulants are artificial; this one is absolutely natural. All other stimulants are poisons; this one is food. All others have reactions, are finally narcotics and depressants; this one has no reactions. Reaction only appears in its absence, when it is lost or wasted.

It is courage, wit, sparkle, radiance, imagination, high spirits, enthusiasm, creative-passion, religious fervor—everything that lifts life above the clod and the monotonous levels. It is the inspiration, directly or indirectly, of almost every poem, song, painting, or other work of art. It has led more men to battle than any bugle note or national peril. It is the great kindler and sustainer of ideals.

Very few understand this or realize it sufficiently. It is commonly observed how lovers glow and radiate and move in an enchanted world; but this is all attributed to love itself. On the contrary, it is the wine of sex that gives love its enchantment and divine dreams. This is easily proven by giving lovers unrestricted license to express their transports. No sooner have they wasted the wine of sex by

126

reckless embraces—often a single orgasm will thus temporarily demagnetize the man—though they love each other just the same, as they will each stoutly assert—the irresistible attraction and radiance and magnetic thrills are gone, and there is a strange drop into cool, critical intellection or indifference, or perhaps dislike. But as the wine of sex reaccumulates and lifts again in the glass, the old magic and charm reappear.

And in this is a clear, natural lesson as to the inestimable value of this elixir in human life and in the ethics of the love-life itself. The one thing that makes life worth living is not its cold facts, but the romantic glow and glamour with which a vivid and kindled imagination invests them, and any manner of conducting the love-life which can create and maintain this zest and charm at its highest is clearly the ethical one. Ascetics, perceiving only that the sex forces give inspiration and that orgasms waste them, and wrongly arguing that in sex-life sexual waste is inevitable, teach that the sexes should avoid each other and turn all sex forces into channels of ambition, public service, religion, etc. This is like telling a man that he should give all his money for the public good, but should avoid earning any; fails to recognize that it takes sexual consciousness, sexual association to develop sexual force. Others, going a step further, getting a glimmer of this last, urge that the sexes associate, but Platonically only. These fail to see that to hold a delicious cup constantly to the lips of a thirsty man and yet forbid him to drink is to waste his force in needless cravings and foolish battles to subdue them and finally usually ends in failure and a sickening sense of guilt.

On the other hand, to have frequent orgasmal embraces, as most married lovers do, is to keep the wine in the sexual lovers low by constant spilling, to thus kill all romance and delight and finally starve and tire out love itself.

Here comes in the application and immense value of Karezza. It is perfect self-control, and yet, once understood and rightly practiced, it is such a perfect and complete satisfaction to all the nerves and appetites concerned that all sense of denial or restriction is lost in one of higher, larger, sweeter expression. It brews and fills every vessel with the sexual wine of ambition, charm, enchantment, as nothing else can and maintains it steadily at a high tide, preventing all losses by preventing all reaction, thus making life continuous romance, genius, and joy.

It avoids alike the waste of starvation and the waste of excess, the wastefulness of self-torture and self-battle to overcome a perfectly natural and wholesome hunger for sexual contact and closeness. It not only avoids all these wastes, it cultivates the grape and presses the wine into the cup of life, which is alone capable of giving man normal inspiration and poetic happiness.

CHAPTER 9

The Karezza Method

Whoso would succeed with Karezza must begin with the mental and spiritual values. Both the man and the woman, and perhaps especially the woman, must resolve that they do not wish the orgasm—that there is a greater spiritual and physical unity and emotional bliss to be obtained without it, besides the sense of safety. This must be the fixed thought and ideal of Karezza.

If you are novices, choose a time when you can both be all alone, unhurried and free from interruptions. Concentrate yourselves entirely on your love and joy and the blending of yourselves into one.

Let the room be warm, the surroundings pleasant and esthetic, and be as unhampered by clothing as possible. Let both of you think more about your love than your passion; translate your sex-passion as much as possible into heart-passion; be sensitively alive to the charm of each other's forms, tones, touch and fragrances; let the thought of mutual tenderness and blessing never leave you for an instant, and make everything that you do and say and feel and think religious in its purity, idealism, aspiration. If you do not come nearer heaven in this act and relation than in anything else you do or ever will do, you fail of perfect Karezza.

Let your embrace be music and a living poem.

Now to you, the man, I speak: Lie down beside your partner and begin to caress her gently with the softness of your hands and fingertips. Tell her to relax herself and lie utterly passive. Tell her to yield herself to the bliss of utter peace and realization. Tell her that you love her and that your whole being longs for entire unity with her. Remember that you cannot use the word "love" too often. She will never tire of it, and it is your watchword. Be to her an incarnate blessing. Try to convey God to her.

As your hands caress her, tell her how beautiful her features are to you—her brow, her hair, her lips, her throat, her arms, hands, bosom, waist, the flowing rounded lines of her legs. Grow eloquent, poetic in her praise. The Loved One can never be too much praised or appreciated by the Lover. Spend plenty of time on these preparatory caresses.

Finally your touch will grow near, and you will come to the focus of all, "the love-flesh"—the Flower. Be tender; be tender, for this is Holiness itself—the seal of God on the woman's person.

If there is dew and moisture here, a flowing with honey, you may begin—that is if your own Finger of Love is firm and fit.

Let there be no hurry or thought of rudeness—be tender, be tender! Have her lie in a straight line, easy, at peace, utterly relaxed and willing.

Begin, seeing to it that the lips do not enfold to prevent. Be gentle, tender, steady, steady. Keep your thoughts on love, not passion. Let her help you by doing the same and murmuring to you, "I love you!" If your passion threatens to overcome you, pause and sublimate it into tenderness of love. Feel strong and confident and say, "I can!" Maintain your own positiveness. Feel yourself stronger than she is, than your passions are. But above all think of your spiritual love. Let her be utterly relaxed physically, let her hold the thought of Peace. Yet for her to hold the thought "I will help him!" would help. Do not worry and do not mind how long you have to wait before strength and self control return and you can go on. Finally the stress subsides and you can continue. If she suffers pain, caress her with your hands, pity her, and be tender and very sympathetic, but reassure her and go on. She herself does not wish you to stop or to fail. Reassure and help each other. When you do finally pass the gates and enter the Hall of the Feast and the Holy of Holies, the worst of the battle will be over and self-control much easier. Penetration can now be perfect and complete.

Now let her put her arms around you and sweetly kiss you, but with heart-love, not yet passion. Pour out your soul to her in extravagance of out-gushing, poetic love. Praise her with every epithet you can honestly use. Give her your soul's best, always your best—and call out the best and purest from her.

At other times—and this is most important—be silent and quiet, but try to feel yourself a magnetic battery, with the Finger of Love as the positive pole, and pour out your vital electricity to her and consciously direct it to her womb, her ovaries, her breasts, lips, limbs, everywhere filling her in every nerve and fiber with your magnetism, your life, love, strength, calmness and peace. This attitude of magnetation is the important thing in Karezza—its secret of sweetest success. In proportion as you acquire the habit and power of withdrawing the electric qualities from your sexual stores and giving them out in blessing to your partner from your sex-organs, hands, lips, skin, everywhere; from your eyes and the tones of your voice; will you acquire the power to diffuse and bestow the sex-

glory, envelop yourselves in its halo and aura, and to satisfy
yourself and satisfy her without an orgasm. Soon you will
not even think of self-control, because you will have no
desire for the orgasm, nor will she. You will both regard it
as an awkward and interrupting accident. And the practice
of Magnetation will beautify and strengthen every organ in
your body that you thus use to express it, as well as hers. It
is the great beautifier. Every look from your eyes, yes,
every touch of your hands, and the tones of your voice will
become vibrant with magnetic charm.

And while you are magnetizing her, try to feel your
utter unity with her. This is the real ideal and end of
Karezza. You will finally enter into such unity that in your
fullest embrace you can hardly tell yourselves apart and can
read each other's thoughts. You will feel a physical unity as
if her blood flowed in your veins, her flesh were yours. For
this is the Soul-Blending Embrace.

If any part of her is weak or ill you can direct the
magnetic currents there with the conscious thought of
healing.

But this is anticipation and a description of the perfect
thing. Perhaps at first you will have much difficulty and
many failures. If while you are penetrating you feel the
orgasm irresistibly approaching, withdraw entirely, lift
yourself a little higher up and have the emission against her
body, while you are pressed close to her warmth and
consoling love. After all is over, wipe all away, carefully,
with a convenient cloth, and be very careful that no drops
can reach her entrance. Then repose quietly by her side,
talking tenderly and lovingly. Do not worry—all will come
right. This is only a common accident with beginners and
to be expected—perhaps with the very passionate and fully-
sexed, several times in succession. Remember you are not

yet used to each other or in magnetic rapport. If she is a true woman she will never reproach you, but will be all patience, sympathy, loyally working with you to attain the perfect result.

At the end of an hour, not sooner, all discharges having long since passed and dried up, if you can again feel potent it will be safe to renew the attempt. (To facilitate this— immediately after the emission stroke, with a firm, gentle pressure, upward from the anus to the scrotum, thus aiding complete discharge, and thereafter soon urinate.)

Caress her for a while, exactly as at first, and be sure her nectar-moisture and willingness are as at first. This is your sign of invitation—of her blissful welcome and Nature's chrism. If she is dry, you will hurt her. The top having been taken off your passion by the emission, you will probably, this time, feel less pressure and be able to easily succeed, but the second testicle may demand equal privileges and again you may fail. Do exactly as at first and so continue till you do succeed. Practice makes perfect, and "It's dogged that does it," as Thackeray said. Never permit yourself to contemplate anything but ultimate and ideal success. It is right here, after one or two failures, that most men give up and declare the whole thing impossible. Yet it is right here, and after such failures, that success becomes easiest, because the discharges have lessened the seminal pressure. If the attempt is renewed just as often as potency can be renewed, success is certain. Any man can succeed if he will persevere.

When you have fully acquired the power you will go on from strength to strength. You will amaze yourself and your partner by what is easily possible to you. You will be able to make any motion you please, that anybody can make anywhere, yet with no failures. You can take the most unusual positions and change places with your partner. You can allow her to be as active as she pleases, or to have the orgasm herself, if she greatly desires it, with no danger to your equilibrium. You can continue the embrace for half an hour, an hour, or even two hours. You can repeat it twice, or perhaps three times, in twenty-four hours, with no sensation of excess. And, so on. But keep the spiritual on top, dominant—loving is the first thing, and at-one-ment in the highest fruition of your souls, your real end. Sex-passion as an end in itself will degrade you. Make it a tool of your spirit.

Karezza is the embrace—The Embrace—the most perfect and satisfying thing in human life, between two mates who truly love. All other caresses point to this and are unsatisfactory because they are not it. It is the only embrace for the truly refined and poetic, as an adequate expression of their insatiable longing to be at one. It is Heaven, on earth.

CHAPTER 10

The Woman's Part in Karezza

The opinion prevails that in Karezza the man does it all and the woman's co-operation is negligible. This error may have arisen in part from the old name, "Male Continence," for the method.

On the contrary, her cooperation, or at least acquiescence, is indispensable, and it is probable that a reckless woman, or one who deliberately and skillfully seeks to do so, can break the control of the most expert man in the art.

For instance, very sudden and unexpected leaps, plunges, or contortions on the woman's part, or wild and abandoned writhings are difficult to withstand, and there is one particular movement, in which the feminine organs clasp tenaciously their sensitive guest and then are drawn suddenly, powerfully backward and downward, which, if executed quickly and voluptuously enough and repeated, I feel sure must unlock the strongest man living.

Also where the woman's muscles are tense and she is quivering and vibrating within with avid hunger almost past control, radiating a thrilling excitement—to attempt entrance at such a moment almost certainly means an explosion, though the same condition after penetration is perfect and a harmonious rapport established, may be supportable, safe and exquisitely delightful, provided the man's own will or passion is still stronger.

Karezza should always begin gently. Too intense or excited a condition on either side, but especially on the woman's side, at the very outset, militates against success. As a rule the woman, at first, should be in a state of complete muscular relaxation. Strong passion in her feeling is not only permissible but excellent, if it is under complete control, if the muscles are not tensed by it, and if it is wisely and helpfully wielded. There is a passion which grips and dominates its subject, greedy, jerky, avid and, as it were, hysterical—like the food-appetite which bolts its meal. This makes Karezza impossible. But there is another passion just as strong or stronger, more consciously delightful, in which the emotion is luxurious, voluptuous, esthetic, epicurean, which lingers, dallies, prolongs, and appreciates, which is neither hurried nor excited, and which invites all the joys and virtues to the feast. This is the passion of true Karezza, especially of the woman who is perfect in the art. She is then to her lover like music, like a poem, not like a bacchante or a neurotic.

As a rule the woman's passion, however great, must be subordinated to the man's. He must feel himself the stronger and more positive of the two and as controlling the situation. If the woman takes the lead, is more positive, especially if she assumes this suddenly and unexpectedly, the result is almost always failure. The woman may rule in the house, in the business, in the social life, and it may be very well, but in Karezza the man must be her chief and her hero, or the relation leaves both dissatisfied. In the ordinary, orgasmal, procreative embrace, the woman may dominate and be successful, at least become impregnated, though her pleasure is usually imperfect, but Karezza is a different matter. And this is because in Karezza the woman is happy in proportion to her fulfilled femininity, the man in proportion to his realized masculinity, and each happy in realizing this in the intimate touch of the other.

There is a physical help which the woman may render at the very outset which is important. It often happens at the beginning of penetration that the labia, one or both of them, are infolded, or pushed in, acting as an impediment and lessening pleasure or causing a disagreeable sensation. If the woman, before penetration begins, will, with her fingers, reach in and open wide the lips, drawing them upward and outward the fullest extent, she will greatly facilitate entrance, and if she will several times repeat this during the Karezza, each time drawing the inner labia outward, while her partner presses inward, it will be found greatly to increase the contact surface and conscious enjoyment, giving a greater sense of ease and attainment.

If a woman by intuitional genius or acquired skill does the right thing, her passion is a food and a stimulus to the man, filling him with a triumphant pride. He is lifted, as it were, by a deep tide, on which he floats buoyantly and exultantly, like a seabird on a wave. Under such conditions both parties become exalted by an enthusiasm approaching ecstasy, a feeling of glorious power and perfect safety no words can adequately describe. And this, I insist, depends mainly on the woman.

Under such conditions of realized power and ability almost any movements, on either side, are possible, provided they are ordinary, expected, and carrying a sort of rhythm. Remember that Karezza is, in its way, a form of the dance. But no movement should be too often repeated without a break. Change is in every way pleasing and desirable. Steady repetition excites to the orgasm, or tires, satiates, chafes, or bruises. No movement at any time should be jerky or unexpectedly sudden. Lawless, nervous, unregulated flouncings and wrigglings should be barred as from a waltz. They properly belong to epileptic states of the orgasmal embrace, and for that very reason have no place in Karezza, which is the opposite. There should be often, long, tender, restful pauses—alternations of "storm and peace," as one woman happily phrased it—and in many cases the whole embrace may most helpfully be very quiet. This part should be decided by the woman and as she wishes it.

The mental attitude and atmosphere and the words of the woman are of inestimable importance. As before said, she must hold the thought that she does not wish or will the orgasm and that she will help the man to avoid it. She should feel calm, strong, confident, safe, and pure. At such a time, a sensitive man will almost know her thoughts and participate in her emotions, and her sub-consciousness and his affect each other like mingling streams. Nervousness, doubt, remorse, suspicion, irritation, guilt, coldness, repulsion, or blame may make him impotent for the time. Too tense or avid a passion may do the same, or pull the trigger of discharge. Her attitude should always, consistently, be one of encouragement. The sudden, perhaps subconscious fear that the woman is expecting more than he can give, and will blame him if he fail, often quite destroys a sensitive man's courage and makes temporary impotence or an emission inevitable, where admiration and approval could develop a sexual hero. Nothing else can possibly help a man so much as to feel all around him the glow of his loved one's loving admiration and trust, her comfort, satisfaction and confidence. Her praise is iron and wine to him.

She need not say much, but if there are few words they must be eloquent. Some women make little, inarticulate musical sounds of applause and joy. Any way she must make him understand, and the chief thing to understand is that the love-side is of a thousand times more importance to her than the sex-side—and this especially if, for the time, he has failed.

There is probably no place in the love-life where an attitude and effort of generous love—a soul-cry of "I will help him! I will praise him! I will love him!" will return so much in personal profit and pleasure to the woman as right here.

The woman must feel innocent—that she is doing right. To accept an embrace under conditions of moral self-reproach may sicken a sensitive partner as well as herself, and cause him genital injury.

Remember that Karezza is passionate emotion guided by the intellect and sweetened by the sanction of the soul. It is an art and belongs to the world of the beautiful. It is because it is so controlled and sanctioned that it appeals so to the higher minds—the noble, the poetic and the refined. Exactly as music and poetry exploit some emotional episode in beautiful detail of rhythmic expression long drawn out, so Karezza exploits, in the rhythmic, changeful figures of a clinging dance, the beauty and bliss of the sexual episode.

Karezza is the art of love in its perfect flower, its fulfillment of the ideal dream.

CHAPTER 11

The Woman's Time of Great Desire

The desire of a woman is seldom so comparatively constant and steady as with a man, but fickle and variable, often latent, though the practice in Karezza tends to equalize the sexes in this. But there are times when, from various reasons, a wave of intense craving suddenly sweeps over her. Particularly is this likely to happen just before the appearance of the menses. And at such times, the woman's desire is very likely to exceed in wild, fiery force that of an ordinary man. Wherefore it follows that very few women at such times get complete satisfaction, leading to great disappointments and marital unhappiness. The unexpected violence of the woman's emotion upsets the man's nerves and causes either a "too quick" orgasm or complete psychic impotence.

Now I think the Karezza-man seldom has any difficulty with the woman whose desire he has himself aroused by caresses and wooing. But when the desire arises spontaneously in her, her natural tendency appears to be to abandon herself to it, to abdicate all self-control, forget everything else, and recklessly, fiercely, almost madly demand sensual gratification. This attitude is a very difficult one indeed for the Karezza-lover to meet because just in proportion to his fineness, sensitiveness, and real fitness to be a Karezza artist is his susceptibility, almost to telepathy, to the woman's moods. If he meets her on her own plane, the orgasm cannot be refused, while if he struggles against her for his Karezza ideal, he is almost certain in the conflict either to lose his poise or to become impotent. This is because this wild desire on her part is normally related to reproduction and is intended by Nature to overcome any male scruples and lead to an immediate embrace and swift orgasm, followed by conception. If, however, the woman wills to have it met on the Karezza plane and converted into an esthetic love-embrace, then she herself must take the initiative and put it on that plane. She must begin the process by getting an inclusive grip on herself, relaxing her tense muscles and steadying her quivering nerves. And no longer concentrating altogether on the sexual, she must sublimate a portion of her passion into heart-love, into a tender desire to encourage her lover and assist him to complete success. The man, whose nerves have been thrown into agitation by her ungoverned attitude and thrilling vibrations, will recover courage and assurance the moment he senses the aid of her self-control, and his proud power will return when her eyes turn admiringly upon him, and her tone and her touch give him her confidence and the cooperating support of her strength.

The wise woman, skillful and trained in her art, will thus beautifully control herself until the man has attained complete and deepest union with her, and the blending current of their mutual magnetism is smoothly running, and then will gradually, as he can bear it, turn on her batteries full strength, reinforcing and redoubling his, till all need of restraint disappears and she may let herself go to her uttermost of bliss and expression, to the limit of complete satiety.

No other time affords an embrace so completely satisfying to the woman as this, so full of joy to both, capable of reaching such heights of ecstasy. But to realize this, she must understand that it is up to her to furnish her full half or more in skillful assistance and magnetic contribution. A woman should be ashamed to expect the man alone to be the Karezza-artist. She should take pride in her own superb sex-power, the poetry of her rhythms, the artistry of her acts. She should have an exulting delight in proving herself worthy of his adoration as the Queen of Love.

And always this should be remembered: The more heart-love, the more sex-joy.

CHAPTER 12

Does the Woman Need the Orgasm?

A lady physician of my acquaintance thinks that a woman would be left congested in her sexual organs, probably, by Karezza, did she not have the orgasm, and the result would finally be disease.

I have not found it so in practice, and the criticism would almost appear to have come from one who had not known Karezza in its perfect form. If valid, it would apply to the man as well and would destroy all force of the case for Karezza for either sex, which is far from what my critic desires.

In Dr. Max Huner's *Disorders of the Sexual System*, a work in which the woman's need of the orgasm is strongly insisted on, I find these significant words: "Whenever a woman states that she remains dry after coitus, it generally means a lack of orgasm." In other words, it is very common in the ordinary orgasmal embrace for the man to have an orgasm in a few moments and depart, leaving the woman entirely unsatisfied in every way. The ordinary husband-and-wife embrace, anyway, is purely sexual and based on his demand to get rid of a surplus. There is little or no thought to make it esthetic or affectional—it is merely animal. If the husband stays long enough and excites his wife sufficiently to have an orgasm, then she has a gushing out of fluids that relieves the congestion brought on by his approaches, and on the physical plane, at least, she is relieved and satisfied, the same as he. If not, "she remains dry." Her moisture or dryness, then, are a pretty good index of her physical satisfaction and relief of congestion, or the reverse.

But what happens in Karezza? Here, if she really loves her partner, her whole nature is attuned to his, in delicious docility, expectation and rapport. Every nerve vibrates in sweet gratitude and response to his touch. There is a marvelously sweet blending and reconciliation of the voluptuous and the spiritual that satisfies both her body and her soul at once and makes her exquisitely sensitive to everything poetic or esthetic in his acts. In this state, when interrelation has been successfully established and his magnetism is flowing through her every fiber, uniting them as one, such a heavenly ecstasy of peace, love and happiness possesses her that she "melts" (there is no other word for it), her whole being wishes to join with his, and though there is no orgasm in the ordinary definition of the word, yet her fluids gush out in an exactly similar manner, and all possible congestion is utterly and completely relieved. Not only is this true of the mucus membranes, but the outer skin also is bathed in a sweet sweat. Indeed, I consider mutual perspiration as very desirable, if not almost indispensable, to the most perfect magnetation, as the moist bodies in loving contact seem to communicate the magnetic, electric currents so much more effectually then.

Rest assured that no woman who has known Karezza in its ideal, its "Heaven" and "Peace" form, remains dry, nor is she left with any trace of congestion or restlessness. On the contrary, she often sinks into a blissful slumber in the very midst of the embrace, just after its sweetest delights.

In truth I have often thought that a very plausible argument might be advanced for the claim that in Karezza, the woman really did have an orgasm, only in such a very gradual form, spread over so long a time, and so sweetly sublimated and exalted in love, that the usual symptoms did not appear or were unrecognized as such.

CHAPTER 13

The Woman's Shock

One who has read the preceding wishes to know why I have said nothing concerning the woman's shock when the man has a failure and is compelled to withdraw.

Perhaps it would be well to consider this, for it is quite true that in some cases the woman feels nervously shocked when the man has to suddenly stop everything and come away. Indeed, in some cases she becomes furiously angry and upbraids him bitterly and in others is sullen, or cold, or dully depressed. She may have backache or headache as a consequence.

But the thing all should know is that many women never feel this way at all but accept the man's failure with a tender amiability and sympathy for him, and carry the whole thing off so sweetly and lovingly that it is clearly seen to be the trivial accident which it truly is. These do not seem to be shocked, or to suffer, and soon restore and woo the lover back to his normal passion and ability, thus helping themselves as much as him.

Now the cause and remedy here can be instantly revealed if we remember that in Karezza all hinges on love. Karezza is easy and successful just in proportion to the abundance of mutual love—hard and difficult just in proportion as mere sex-craving dominates love. If the woman loves her mate so much that his mere presence, voice, touch, are a heaven of joy to her, so much that the sex-relation is only an adjunct and she could be happy if entirely without it, then, by a sort of paradox, not only does she enjoy it twice as exquisitely as her merely sex-craving sister, but can let it go at any moment without a pang. On the other hand the more the man rises above mere sex-hunger in delicious perfection of romantic love, the more easy and natural and effortless becomes Karezza-control, and the less likely is he to have a failure; and the more the woman loves him, almost to forgetting of sex, the more she assists him to be perfect in sex-power and control, while the less she cares if he does fail. In every way and on every side, absence of love, or a break in the tender stream of romantic rapport and adoration and soul-blending, makes the mechanical technique of Karezza difficult, awkward, unsatisfactory or impossible.

Remember this: If a woman does not love her man with heart or soul, or at least an innocent sense of need that arouses in her a tender gratitude for his service, but merely craves sex-sensation, her avid and animal passion, sensed by his sexual nerves on contact, will arouse in him a lust as soulless as her own, or will render him impotent, or will give him an initial power and then demand so imperiously of his centers that denial and control will be impossible and helplessly he will fail. Just so, if he comes to her only for her sex, not in tender love or sympathy, he will find he cannot hold.

It is the predominance of the finer emotions, the capture of the body by the soul and the joyous devotion of every function to that dear service, that alone renders Karezza easy and divinely satisfying.

The woman who is shocked in this case is one who loves less than she should; the shock is disappointment of sex-craving, and when she embraces a man whom she loves more than sensation she will never feel it.

CHAPTER 14

Psychic Impotence

This book would be incomplete were I to make no mention of that sudden and mysterious loss of erectile power which sometimes befalls men. Perhaps there are few men who do not know the secret dread of some day becoming impotent.

I remember a champion athlete—a magnificent man physically—confessing to me that he was afraid to marry, fearing that he would not be able to satisfy his wife. And perhaps the earliest sexual story that I remember was that of a soldier, in the time of the Civil War, who by a sudden and natural motion lost his power, which no effort of himself or his mistress could restore. All my life such tales have come to me. Tragic tales, some of them, as where a spiteful woman overwhelmed her helpless lover with shame and reproach; where divorce was demanded for this cause; where a marriage between two devoted lovers remained unconsummated to the end, the husband dying in a few years, perhaps of a broken heart. These and many others. Who has not heard of the pitiful case of Carlyle and his Jane Welsh, as told by Froude? And it has been hinted that the same cause lay back of Ruskin's beautiful surrender of his wife to the artist Millais, and of the relation of Swift to his Stella and Vanessa.

The mystery of this thing lies in its suddenness and unaccountability. No wonder that in the superstitious it has suggested witchcraft. If it came only to cowards, to weaklings, to the sterile, to bashful boys and inexperienced lovers, it would not be so strange. But precisely these may never be troubled by it, while a Don Juan of experience and proud list of conquests. A hero of courage or a Titan of genius, whose virile mind dominates his time, may suddenly be stricken by it, perhaps blasted for life. It may occur with one woman and not with another, at one time and not another, or it may appear permanent and incurable.

The very worst of it is the mental effect upon the victim. For ages the man human has dreaded to be called "impotent." His manly power is the dearest attribute of man. There are no words to describe the agony, the shame, the bitter self-reproach, the helplessness, the awful despair; that may overwhelm an innocent, loving, and otherwise perfect man when the fear comes upon him that his virility has left him and that he may perhaps always disappoint and appear a weakling in the eyes of the woman whose embraces may be dearer and more desired than aught else in life. Just as nothing else gives a man such pride, courage, inspiration, and exaltation as to be able to perfectly embrace and satisfy the woman he loves, so nothing else has such power to crush, sadden, sicken, and embitter a man as sexual failure. It drives many and many a man to solitude, old-bachelorhood, misanthropy, misogyny, insanity, or suicide. How much of the bitterness and gall of Carlyle's writings may have come from this and the agony of his volcanic and morbid soul under its torture, who can tell?

Now because of the sufferings of my sex from this cause and, incidentally, of the women who love them, I have written this chapter. And it is because I wish to speak a helping word that I preface it with the frank confession (which I would otherwise dread to make) that I have myself, at different times and places, suffered enough from this nervous inability to give me a vivid glimpse of its tortures and a true sympathy with its victims. Even a very few and fleeting experiences can do this. Therefore I have studied it, with a personal as well as general interest. And believe my conclusions are of value.

And first I want to correct many common misconceptions. Psychic impotence, though of course not normal, is not pathologic. It is not a proof of ill health. It is not an evidence of weakness, even of sexual weakness. I speak positively when I say that the man completely impotent at night may be absolutely potent in the morning, or vice versa, the man who fails with one woman may within the hour be a marvel of manly power with another. It is not a proof of a lack of love but often of the opposite. It is not in the least an evidence of sterility. A man quite sterile may have no trace of psychic impotence and the man troubled by it may be most virile. I knew a man who completely failed with his wife for some nine or ten months after marriage, who finally became the father of four children and is now a grandfather. It is not a proof of inexperience, for it may occur at any time to any man, after any number of years' experience. Thus Forel says, "It is often produced suddenly at the time of marriage in persons who have hitherto been very capable, even in Don Juans." I knew a widower, the father of two children, who married a second time, found himself impotent, and never overcame it with that woman. At the time of his death, his wife, though she had been that for years (and their life otherwise was most loving) was still a virgin.

So let no man shame himself for this thing, and let no woman despise her lover for it.

Whatever it is, it depends nearly always upon the action and reaction of the two natures brought together upon each other when in a state of sexual nervousness, or upon some strong mental or subjective impression, checking or diverting the normal nerve stimulus which causes the potent expression of manly power. Thus even with those already in successful embrace, a keenly enjoyed joke, a startling sound from without, an argument, an angry word, or a preoccupying conversation, may suddenly and completely cut off the current.

But usually it seems to arise from autosuggestion or from some suggestions derived, unconsciously or consciously, from the woman. I say "unconsciously" because I am persuaded that there is much that passes between two lovers of which their brains and conscious egos know nothing. I am inclined to believe that there is a telepathy and clairvoyance between their subjective minds and even between their sexual systems of which their consciousness takes no note. I am satisfied that the sexual nature of the woman may love a man when her mind is convinced that she does not love him—that her sex may desire him while her heart refuses. She may feel an almost irresistible impulse to yield herself to a man whom her soul fears and loathes. Or she may love a man mentally, spiritually, even with a heart-love, to whom her sex is cold and indifferent. Human life is nowadays very complex.

And this is why it is that the most sensitive, refined, intuitive men are the most likely to suffer from psychic impotence. The coarse, sensual, selfish man, concerned only with his own passions and their glut, is little likely to feel it. The man who asks only opportunity, not consent, the man who can rape, is safe from it. But the man who reverences womanhood, the man who adores his mistress, the man deeply and passionately in love, so that every thought and suggestion from his loved one sways him like a compelling power, is easily overcome. We must remember that there is probably no time when a strong man is so utterly suggestible as when he is completely in love. His whole nature is then melted, sensitive, impressible (especially by Her) to a degree otherwise impossible with him.

This is why usually coarse men temporarily exalted by a great love may spend a whole evening in the close companionship of a beloved and reverenced woman and never consciously think of sex. This is why a man hitherto perfectly successful with prostitutes and voluptuous women (who appeal only to sex-passion), when he comes to the bridal-bed with some shrinking and nervous and spiritual girl, who knows nothing of sex and to whom the heart love is everything, may suddenly find his sex efforts imperfect. The very nervousness and fright of his companion, her ignorance, her excitement, her dread of the unknown thing about to happen—all this may react on a man and quite unnerve him, and all the more in proportion to his real love for and rapport with her. Often at such a time, the excitement, fatigue, and dread of the girl have taken away all sex desire from her, and she only fears being hurt, and this sex negativeness may infect her lover subconsciously and demagnetize him. Even where the beginning is all right, a single cry of pain from the bride may unman the groom. How can he go on and hurt her!

A woman should know that impotence is often the greatest proof a man can offer of the depth, purity, and spirituality of his love for her, of his tenderness and consideration and of the probability of his being a life-long lover.

For we must remember that heart-love, spiritual love, that dear and tender at-one-ing and companioning which romantic love now idealizes and desires, represents an evolution. The original love was simply fierce sexual passion, hungry, physical, selfish, concerned only with its own gratification. And to this day, these two loves are generally combined in very various degrees, with the coordination between them by no means perfect. It is often difficult to get just the right balance and proportion and requires the wise cooperation of both, something not likely to occur at first—especially in the new, strange conditions of a first conjugation between hitherto sexual strangers, particularly if the woman has for many years known nothing of or repressed the sex-life and has become moody, abnormal, and hypersensitive, or lacks normal sensation, or if the man is very sensitive and deeply in love. There is likely to occur an unbalance and dislocation of the sexual elements with strange results.

Very often it would be better if, for the first night, or for many nights, there was no effort made toward sexual congress, but only toward full expression of the caressive heart-love, until such time as both were consciously ripe and could no longer be denied.

The great danger of an initial failure with a nervous, sensitive and impressible man, is that he may be seized with panic, a terror that the heaven opening to him may be closed forever; that his dear one must be disappointed; that she may despise and cease to love him, perhaps even come to loathe him; or that he must live on under the shame of her pity and unsatisfied longings; that his masculine fellows may come to know of it and ridicule him as no man—and all the other terrors that an excited imagination can conjure up; and that this fear and conviction may be stamped in and fixed by autosuggestion upon his subconsciousness, making his fear a fact. Sometimes the counter-suggestion of hypnotism, in these cases, becomes the only cure.

One of the most mysterious variants of this trouble is where the woman's desire is unusually, perhaps abnormally strong and passionate, and the man thrilled with an equal desire, finds himself helpless. This is difficult to explain, but I think it will usually be found in these cases that the woman is one who by reason of her changeable moods, previous cruelty, or something of that sort, has produced a subjective fear in the man. In such temperaments, if not immediately answered and satisfied, the woman will sometimes fly into a nervous rage, covering her disappointing partner with shame and, cruel reproach, or withdrawing her favors in cold contempt. Even if not conscious of this fear it may affect a man, or it may exist as a race-memory, and act on his subconsciousness. In some cases, I think the sudden nymphomania of the woman causes disturbed nervous vibrations, which upset the nervous balance of the man. But I admit there are some examples of this form for which I have as yet no explanation. The consoling fact is that this form is usually very ephemeral and occasional only.

Sometimes the heart-love is so strong and motherly in a woman, that the man comes completely under its dominance, and though the two may have great happiness and even sensuous joy in each other's embraces, the local sex-organs fail to become completely aroused. This is particularly likely to happen in a woman no longer young, who is near the turn of life, and is quite normal.

Now as the causes of this thing are mostly psychic, so should the remedies be. Nourishing diet, especially of shellfish, milk, eggs, may assist. Running, horseback riding, and muscle-beating over the lower spine, nates, hips, thighs, and abdomen, by way of a local tonic, with abundant sleep can all help. But the chief need is to establish the right relation between the psychic natures of the lovers themselves. Especially does this depend upon the woman. If she is patient, tender, loving, considerate; if she can prove to him that she is so happy in his tenderness, his unity, his devotion, that the sex-union is really a very secondary and comparatively unimportant matter with her, and she can wait any necessary time for its consummation without distress; especially if she daintily and wisely cultivates in herself a touch of the coquettish, sensuous, voluptuous—appealing subtly and luxuriously to his passions and their stimulus—success is seldom long in coming.

There is nothing that so arouses, supports, and sustains the normal sex-passion in a man as for a strongly-sexed woman to fill her aura toward him with a strong, steady, self-controlled appeal—tender, loving, admiring, yet deliciously sensuous, and esthetically voluptuous; pure, yet deep, warm, alluring. To most men this is an instant and permanent cure. The lover is lifted as a strong swimmer is by some deep and briny tide, and floats deliciously at ease, bathed in bliss, and in the consciousness of perfect power.

But a nervous, hysterical, moody woman—now frantic, now frigid—often plays strange pranks with the sex-power of a susceptible man.

And the man must, whatever happens, maintain his courage, self-respect, and faith in his own manhood, and love and work wisely on till the tide comes in.

More and more as man becomes less dominating, less simply carnal, more sensitive, refined and at one with the woman he loves will power to initiate, direct, and sustain his sex-life and love-expression, to make, mar, or mold him emotionally be hers. And woman should be very glad that this is so. The love-life should be hers. This power is her opportunity, her shield, her glory, and the evidence of the greatness of her soul is in the wisdom of her use of it.

And just as this spot is the most vulnerable in a man's whole life, the place where he can be most deeply and incurably wounded, even so is the depth and eternal quality of his gratitude to the woman who continues to love him despite his weakness and assists him back to pride and power.

I remember one beautiful instance of this that came to my knowledge. A handsome and brilliant young man, weakened in this way, attracted the sympathy of a woman who devotedly called out, cultivated and restored his power. And though she was very plain, a woman of many faults, unpopular, and many years his senior, he adhered to her ever afterward with a faithfulness and gratitude that nothing could mar. He no doubt felt that she had done more than save his life—she had made it worthwhile to live.

CHAPTER 15

Karezza the Beautifier

When the full magnetic rapport of Karezza has been
realized, in which the two souls and bodies seem as one,
supported and floating on some divine stream in Paradise,
all sense of restraint and difficulty gone and succeeded by a
heavenly ease, power, exaltation, pure and perfect bliss,
diffused throughout the entire being, it is then that the eyes
and faces shine as though transfigured. Every tone becomes
music, every emotion poetry. And this normally continues
for a long time, perhaps hours, gently subsiding, finally,
into a sweet, contented lassitude and child-like slumber.
But even to the last moment of consciousness, there is a
most clinging and tender affectionateness and desire to be
close to the loved one, gratitude for the gift of such joy;
nothing of that indifference or revulsion usually concluding
the orgasmal embraces. And this continues after parting,
even for days, so that one walks in a heavenly dream, and
where the embrace is often repeated, tends to become a
fixed and continuous habit, resulting in the most ideal love;
if the parting is permanent, remaining in the memory for
years, causing ever a gentle and tender reminiscence to
pervade the thought of the loved one.

It is because of this that Karezza, though a sex act, so
wonderfully increases and makes enduring the heart love. It
is the embrace of the angels; sex sublimed by soul.

And because of all this it excels all other forces or influences as a beautifier. The faces of those who practice it tend to become exceedingly beautiful, on the spiritual plane especially; that is to say, it is the beauty of expression that is developed, rather than that of feature, though the features surely but more slowly follow, a serene, sweet light in the eye, a delicacy and refinement of line, a radiance and play of feature, a glad timbre in the voice that vibrates an inexpressible magnetism and makes even the plainest personality fascinating.

Owing to the blending of the two natures, their mutual exaltation and reception of each other's moral qualities, it is soon to be noted that lovers who practice Karezza display the fruits of such inspiration and transmutation. The woman becomes strong, proud, confident, logical—displaying the finer masculine—while the man becomes gentle, considerate, compassionate, sympathetic, intuitive — revealing the finer feminine. Thus the sexes spiritually change and interweave and become at one.

Is it any wonder if this most vitalizing of all elixirs, thus habitually fed to them, should make the organs receiving it, or through which it passes, beautiful, magnetic, graceful, radiant with life? Look at the lips, eyes, cheeks of a happy bride and find your answer. Joy is the greatest beautifier on earth, and there is no joy like sex-joy. I prophesy that when Karezza becomes the habit of the people, made easy and perfect by inheritance developing into instinct, that the human race will become beautiful exceedingly, beyond the beauty of all former times; a subtle, inward beauty, shining through. The sex-force, which produces such rapture when felt locally, such a divine ecstasy when diffused in Karezza, will be healing in the hands of the physician, eloquence on

the lips of the orator, fire in the eyes of the leader, genius in
the brain of the great.

CHAPTER 16

The Danger of Excess

The accusation is continually brought against sex-reformers that they become "obsessed by sex" and rush into excess. And this is sometimes deserved, for the tendency to excess exists in every intense nature toward whatever activity may predominate in interest.

But it is no condemnation of any pursuit to prove that it may be indulged in to excess. Its merit or demerit must be shown quite aside from the behavior of its advocates. For excess manifests itself everywhere. Nothing can be imagined more innocent than useful labor, intellectual study, or the desire for safety, yet every day we observe men ruined by overwork, blind or neurasthenic from over-study, or cowardly or weak from excess of caution. Most of the accusers of excess in sex are religious, yet excess in religion, leading to bigotry, fanaticism, religious insanity, is among the very commonest forms of abnormality. To seek physical perfection is certainly most praiseworthy, yet few athletes escape an overstrain in training or competition that damages or kills.

It is common to praise "love" in opposition to sex, but love, so far as it exists apart from sexual expression, is peculiarly prone to excessive manifestation. Maternal love is perhaps the typical and purest form, yet in almost every mother we see her love become over-indulgent, partial and blindly unjust. The jealousy almost always present in the deepest loves, no matter how spiritual, proves excess, and when love is denied or suddenly withdrawn, unhealthful, insane or criminal symptoms almost always supervene, requiring all the powers of the spirit to quell. With every virtue known to man the same is true. In proportion to the power of any faculty, or the richness and value of any emotion, is the peril of excess. And sex shares this danger with the rest.

The reproach of excess, in many cases, is the result of mere prejudice. There is still an immense amount of theological odium attached to sex in the popular mind. It is a thing apart, to be kept secret and mentioned with bated breath, a thing doubtful and suspicious, if not certainly vile. To those who think thus, all frank interest in and attention to sex is excessive. And there is another large class who have themselves only abnormal interest in sex, knowing it only from experience of lust. To them all interest in sex borders on debauch. A man who studies sex or writes on sex is sure to be denounced by such people as "obsessed by sex." Yet there is no more reason why a sexologist should not devote himself to the study and elucidation of sexual phenomena than there is why an astronomer should not study stars or a geologist rocks.

But as sex is interwoven with our deepest feelings, the fountainhead of some of our strongest emotions, it is certainly liable to excess, and far be it from me to deny this. There is a very real peril that those who are very loving and strongly sexed may give too much of themselves to the absorbing concerns of passion. A due proportion and balance is necessary in everything.

It is perfectly true that the wine of sex may sometimes go to the head and lead to a preoccupation with sex bordering on satyriasis or nymphomania, just as any other passion may become an emotional intoxication. Love and sex are subject to the universal laws of excess and satiation. Love and the thrill of sex are delightful feelings and we strive to hold them and intensify—this is natural and right within reason, but if continued too long the inevitable result is that the nerves become powerless to appreciate or respond. We may drain the reserves of the other faculties by diverting them all to sex—may thus indirectly weaken and atrophy them and finally may end by devitalizing love and sex themselves. And lovers are prone to spend time and money lavishly on their delight and may thus waste. Loss of sleep is a common source of love-waste too little considered. And in the man there are often the crude losses of the orgasm. There may be a feverish state of the system developed in which appetite and digestion are impaired and application or effective work become impossible; or an abnormal loneliness, destroying appreciation of or contentment with the usual joys of life.

Uxoriousness, or slavish devotion and idolatrous admiration, may cause one partner to abdicate vindication of selfhood and spoil the beloved.

Those who are weak or moderately developed in sex may be less in danger, nevertheless it is to be remembered that the weak person may be overdone by an amount of expression that would be nothing to a stronger one. Excess is an individual matter which each should observe from the center of his own personality.

Those who practice Karezza are less liable to excess, because spared the waste of the orgasm and because in them the emotion is sublimated and diffused, including soul, body, and mind, the entire selfhood—yet they also may overdo. Excess here is more apt to manifest itself in the form of exhaustion from loss of sleep, or from too prolonged stress of tender emotion, or perhaps merely in the form of diverting too much time from other interests, rightfully precedent. There are cases too, not well understood as yet, in which one party exhausts or demagnetizes the other, perhaps acts consciously or unconsciously as a vampire, or in which both mutually exhaust each other. Such symptoms are sometimes observed by two people merely in each other's presence, with no reference to sex, and are not necessarily coincident with any excess, but belong rather to the department of maladjustments and misfits, yet may unfortunately coexist with a good deal of the finest mutual love.

It is possible to embrace too frequently in Karezza or maintain the embraces too long. Only experience can determine what is moderation and what excess.

Those who do not use Karezza are vastly more liable to excess, and this usually from too frequent and intense orgasms, too frequent pregnancies, or too coarse, cynical and invasive an attitude. Where there is merely a physical itch or craving gratified, with no mutual tenderness or kindness, or perhaps actually against the desire or protest of one party, sex is always excessive.

If there is no indulgence except where there is mutual consent and enjoyment, mutual kindness and consideration, careful regard for the conditions of health and useful living, and a dominant conviction that all physical acts should express beauty of soul, there need be no fear. Excess is only where the act is individually or socially detrimental.

CHAPTER 17

Final Considerations

It will be noticed that I lay great stress upon the value of love in Karezza and of refined feeling. For success, there cannot be too much of both. Great love and poetry of feeling represent the ideal in the practice of the art of love. But I never forget the limitations of real life. Not all people can be poets. And I quite recognize that it often happens that very good people wish to marry or unite their lives because they are lonely or physically starving, who yet have not and never could have any great, mutual, romantic love. The practical question is: Can such successfully or beneficially practice Karezza? Certainly. The mere skeleton or essential framework of Karezza is this: That the parties be honest and kind toward each other, sexually healthy, the woman willing, the man potent, mutually at peace in their consciences about the matter, and united in their desire that there shall be no orgasm on the man's part. On this basis they can succeed and with benefit, but their happiness and peace will be very inferior compared to what it would be if deeper and higher emotions could be included. But when two pure and trustful friends once begin a relation of this kind, it seldom fails to go on to more beautiful attainments. Karezza seems to create inevitably a tendency to caress and be tender. It is a sort of natural marriage ceremony, which marries more and more with every repetition.

In relation to Karezza, the question of the orgasm continually arises. The early writers on male continence, I believe, all argued that the seminal secretion resembled that of the tears, was normally secreted and reabsorbed, and need never be discharged except for procreation. Other physiologists, of a later date, declared that the semen, once secreted, could never be reabsorbed and must find discharge, thus denying those who have contended that reabsorbed semen was what gave the "illusion," the thrill, the virile feeling, the strongly sexed man knows. It is now believed that this inspiring elixir comes from the ductless glands.

It is very well to have a healthy skepticism about science as about theology. The theories and assertions of science too often crumble and fade before our very eyes. What we know from experience and observation in practice is a safer guide. And the practical facts are these: An accumulation of semen does occur in almost every man, sometimes, varying very much with different men, which apparently must have vent. It is a surplus. Either more has been secreted than can be absorbed, or, once secreted, it cannot be absorbed. Anyway it will come out. In the man who has nothing to do with women this causes the "wet dream," which is a perfectly natural way of getting rid of a surplus. In Karezza it causes the occasional failure. At least it is one cause. For no matter how expert the Karezza artist, the occasional failure to restrain the orgasm must be counted on. That beautiful equilibrium between the parties which leaves both so satisfied sometimes fails to occur and the man's orgasm irresistibly approaches, he is obliged to withdraw, and his Karezza becomes a *coitus interruptus*. The success of Karezza appears to depend on the sublimation of mere sex feelings into predominance of love feelings and upon a diffusion of sex-consciousness so that too much is not concentrated locally. If local concentration becomes too great, an explosion inevitably follows. I have observed that if the woman a man loves becomes suddenly cold or angry toward him, this local concentration is very apt to occur. It is more apt to occur with a fickle and moody or coquettish woman than with a steady and deep one; with a weak woman whose passion is fitful than with a strong woman whose great passion lifts and carries her partner on an even tide. It is harder to be continent on a full meal than on an empty stomach; harder soon after a bath. A vivid emotional experience of any kind may cause it, or intense intellectual exercise. The approach of a change in the weather, if sharp and marked, especially a "cold snap," may bring it about. It is all right and not to be worried over. *Coitus interruptus* used to be considered very bad for the man, but the modern view is that it is harmless but may affect the woman nervously by leaving her unsatisfied. But this does not apply to the well-trained Karezza couple because, first, the woman has the relation so frequently and so satisfyingly that she can well afford an occasional lapse; and, second, she knows that in a few hours, perhaps in a single hour, she may have it again, usually rather better than ordinarily, and therefore has no excuse for nervousness. Just as the man must always be kind to the woman and stop the relation at any moment if she grows weary, or for any other reason wishes it, so the woman must be kind to him, cheerful, sweet, and patient if he sometimes fails, and by this calling up of her affectional nature effectually cures the morbid self-pity which might make her nervously ill. Most men feel that they must have the orgasm at certain intervals, and there are scientists who have claimed to have discovered a sexual rhythm or periodicity in man which would seem to support this. But this sexual cycle in man appears to occur from once in four day to once a month, according to the individual. On the other hand, almost all women want intercourse very frequently, and long and leisurely each time, and sexual scientists support this, too. It is admitted also by the highest authorities (they do not know Karezza) that *coitus interruptus* is the surest of all ways to avoid undesired pregnancy, while the contraceptives are none of them safe. Now all these things can be reconciled in Karezza. Let the man learn Karezza, and his wife can have intercourse as often and as long as she likes, while the occasional failure gives him the relief of the orgasm at the time of his "period" or some other time.

And there is the question of the woman's orgasm. It is held by quite a good many men—some women and many physicians say the same—that a woman also needs the orgasm, and that if she does not have it her health suffers. It is also commonly claimed that the woman's orgasm is essential in conception for the best results.

With these contentions I disagree. I consider the female orgasm an acquired habit and not natural. The male needs the orgasm to expel the sperm, but the female has no analogous need—her orgasm has nothing to do with expelling the ovum.

In all the animal embraces I have been able to witness, while the orgasm of the male was evident, I could see no evidence of a female orgasm. If the female orgasm is not necessary and does not occur below woman, why should it be necessary of occur in woman?

"To give her pleasure," is the answer, and a good one, but I hold that if she will have Karezza, she can have a finer, sweeter pleasure without it.

My objections to the female orgasm in Karezza (for it is to be noted that in the original "Male Continence," the woman had the orgasm if she wanted it) are threefold:

That self-control is more difficult for the man where the woman thus indulges herself.

That after her orgasm the woman is less magnetic, enthused and delightful as a partner, enjoys the Karezza less, and quite often soon becomes indifferent, depressed or irritable.

That indulgence in the orgasm on either side cultivates the merely sexual at the expense of the affectional, the romantic, the spiritual.

As I know that a woman who has known the perfect orgasm may deliberately abandon its practice completely in favor of Karezza, on the ground of its being less satisfying than Karezza minus all orgasm, and as I know that women who have never in all their lives had an orgasm may be beautifully satisfied and blissfully happy as well as healthy in Karezza without it, and this more and more as the years go on, I feel that I have good grounds for saying that I believe the orgasm in the woman is entirely unnecessary and artificial and that she is better off without it.

The ordinary male orgasmal embrace seldom satisfies the woman. It is too brief and animal for her. And if she is not satisfied in sex, of course, she suffers. But if she can have the orgasm with it, that gives her a kind of satisfaction, and that is why the orgasm seems beneficial to her, and her physician, seeing the benefit, endorses the act. But the same woman could be better satisfied in the non-orgasmal embrace of perfect and prolonged Karezza, and then the orgasm would be seen to be needless—that is my position.

My objections to the female orgasm in conception are as follows:

When a woman has an orgasm, she has a discharge of vital-force and is left demagnetized, as a man is after an orgasm. I believe she demagnetizes the germ in so doing and that in this state it is less fit for impregnation than if there had been no orgasm—but this may be mere theory.

I believe, too, that the ideal way in the procreative embrace is for the man to waive all attempt at pleasure or to prolong the embrace, but to have his orgasm as quickly and forcefully as possible, directing all his magnetism into the seed and drawing nothing of her vital-force from the woman, but leaving it all for the child, and then to come immediately away and entirely withdraw from the room. The woman is to have no orgasm and to remain after the act quiet and recumbent for an hour or more. This also is theory, but at least I can say that where my advice was asked and followed, pregnancy occurred, where before was sterility.

And this I know, that a woman can conceive without herself having an orgasm. There is every probability, I would say, considering the sexual lives of the average, that the majority of women conceive without it. I believe she conceives more easily and surely without it, for it is reasonable to infer that the spasmodic motions and abdominal contractions of the orgasm would tend to expel the sperm and then leave the parts negative and flaccid, instead of avid and receptive.

I know that a woman can have conception without having an orgasm, have a normal pregnancy and easy parturition, give birth to a perfect child, destined to grow up beautiful and healthy in body and a genius in mind. What more or better can any mother do? There remains the further question of Karezza in pregnancy: I feel sure the woman is better off in pregnancy without the usual orgasmal intercourse. It is liable on the man's part to be too violent and to cause her injury. And for the woman herself to have an orgasm might certainly bring a miscarriage. But on the other hand, I believe an occasional very gentle and quiet and tender Karezza (the man being careful of his weight) is most beneficial to the pregnant woman, and even to the unborn babe which is thus bathed in the magnetic aura and enfolded in the love of both its parents.

The woman feels it a very great comfort to have her husband's love embrace at such a time and often peculiarly longs for it. I have never seen or heard of any bad results from it and I recommend its considerate use.

The advantages of Karezza, as a love-act and otherwise, may be summed up as follows:

It permits the embrace more frequently. It permits full penetration, contact and motion to the fullest extent, with no intervening substance whatever, thus completely satisfying woman's greatest sexual craving, which is for long continued, tender touch, as deep as possible, as long as possible. It gives the slower, more deliberate, more luxurious nature of the woman plenty of time to be fully aroused and fully satisfied. It satisfies her love-nature along with her sex-nature—which to her is the most important thing. It removes all fear of pregnancy, so that she feels safe. It requires no lotions, douches, greases, tampons, plugs, pessaries, drugs, syringes, skin-pockets, rubber bags, napkins, getting up in the cold, or any adjustments whatever—it leaves the poetry of the act not only intact, but intensifies it. Thus it satisfies the imagination, the craving for the ideal. Because it cultivates self-control and requires the sublimation and transmutation of the merely sexual into the tender, the loving, the gentle, the romantic, its inevitable tendency is elevating, not degrading, to redeem and purify sex, not only to maintain its perfect natural innocence, but to add to it the chivalrous, the moral, the religious, in an ascending scale. Thus it satisfies the mind and soul. It gives complete birth control.

A general knowledge and use of it must certainly lift most of the odium which now attaches to everything sexual, thus increasing the respect for and appreciation of sex, its liberty and exercise, thereby automatically removing gradually the curse of social reproach.

Between the well-mated it leaves no sense of weakness or exhaustion, but one rather of sweet satisfaction, fullness of realization, peace, often a physical glow and mental glamour that lasts for days, as if some ethereal stimulant, or rather nutriment, had been received.

As this satisfaction is always normally combined with a grateful affectionateness and tender yearning toward the partner, it maintains, increases, and makes habitual the union.

Where properly and successfully performed between the well-mated, it gives the most absolute and perfect satisfaction without the orgasm.

Withdrawing the sexual electricity from the merely sex-organs, distributing it throughout the system and discharging it from every part toward the loved one, exchanging with that loved one, every part so used is electrified and vitalized and becomes more beautiful— Karezza is the greatest beautifier.

And this satisfaction, joy and perfected love inevitably react to increase the general physical health and mental vigor—Karezza maintains youth and is one of the best of the health exercises.

Appendix

A school of physicians has arisen which claims the orgasm as a most important function, beneficial, and justifiably attained by artificial means if natural ones are not available, including with apparent approval, masturbation and the use of mechanical and chemical contraceptives.

The chief evil of this teaching appears to be that it is calculated to leave the reader of little experience with the idea that orgasms are practically harmless, that excess is unlikely, and that if no immediate bad results are noticed the practice may be indulged in to about the limit of desire.

To understand this problem we must consider the endocrine system.

In the organism, there are ductless glands whose function is to deliver energy. These glands and the varying power of their function, I conceive to have a most intimate relation to the orgasm, its need and nature. Where these glands work excessively, we may have a condition of almost or quite maniacal energy, quite upsetting the usual inhibitions; or, at the other extreme, where their action is deficient, we may have depressions, weakness, melancholy, cowardice, neurasthenia. Sexual love inspires the ductless glands to action, which is one reason why it is so healthful and joy-inspiring. To those who have deficient action of the ductless glands, sexual love becomes most beneficial, giving strength, courage, optimism, because it brings their action up to normal, or nearer to normal. But to a man who has excessive action of the ductless glands, sexual love, or sex-relations, may so increase this that a painful tension is created even a state of emotional intoxication or madness that may be insane.

All sexual crimes, rape, jealous murder, outrages of "Jack-the-Ripper" type, originate in this sexual insanity caused by excessive action of the energy glands—or that is my theory. On the other hand, bashfulness and impotence occur where the endocrine glands do not work strongly, or work fitfully, and give rise to melancholy and an "inferiority complex" before the adored one.

The relation to the orgasm is this: In the normal man, under usual conditions, it may be conceived that the semen secreted is all absorbed as fast as secreted, no surplus accumulates, no pressure is felt. There is a steady, normal output of energy from the ductless glands, neither excessive nor deficient. That the semen can be and is absorbed I think is satisfactorily proven by the numerous instances where men have been sterilized by accident, disease, or intentional operation in such a way that the testicles are left unharmed, but the semen is cut off from its natural outlet. After being once secreted only two things are possible—either it must be absorbed, or it will form a swelling. It does *not* form a swelling; therefore it certainly is absorbed.

And the orgasm is not essentially a discharge of semen, for it is possible for a man to have an orgasm with no discharge of semen, and women, who have no semen, can have orgasms as violently as any man. An orgasm is essentially a violent emotional discharge of energy or nervous force. Fits of rage, weeping, etc. are often truly orgasmal, and in many cases serve as substitutes for sexual orgasms, as in hysterics. Where the ductless glands are excited to more than usual activity, energy accumulates in

174

the nerves and a demand is felt for its discharge. If the thoughts are then sexually excited there will be a demand for a sexual discharge, especially if the excitation has been of a sort to cause the energy to accumulate in the sexual centers, causing congestion. For wherever the nervous energy flows the blood flows also and remains congested unless the energy is discharged or withdrawn.

Now observers report very differently as to after effects of orgasms. Some "feel like a sick dog," or report dizziness, lassitude, weakness, dimness of vision, perhaps vomiting or fainting, while others only feel relaxed and soothed or declare energy and buoyancy increased. Some can endure only one orgasm at long intervals of perhaps a month or more; others glory in daily orgasms or even a number at one interview. Even the same individual often experiences a wide range in power or in good or bad effects. How explain these differences in the testimony of good witnesses? I think an understanding of the ductless glands explains all.

There are those in whom these glands work with more than usual power, and if the energy thus received takes the direction of the genitals for an outlet, such a one feels a tremendous need of an orgasm, and, if he has it, he feels it relieves and benefits him. And if his glands are excited by the sexual embrace, they may rush more energy into the vacuum, even an increased amount, making repetitions possible until the pressure is lowered. During this the contagion, his emotions may excite the glands of the woman, and she also may have multiple orgasms or may have them anyhow because of her own endocrine flow.

On the other hand, a man in whom the flow of endocrines or hormones is only normal may feel quite spent after an orgasm, demagnetized, and must rest before a repetition. If his glandular flow is weak and a surplus only slowly accumulates, then if he repeats too soon, he may spend not only his too scanty surplus, but may draw on his reserves to a degree that may cause uncomfortable or even alarming symptoms.

But must the nervous sexual surplus find an outlet through the orgasm? Yes, say the doctors of the orgasmal school, or health suffers. Here is where I differ. They recognize a *coitus completus*, a *coitus interruptus*, a *coitus reservatus*, and I would add a *coitus sublimatus*, which may also be a *coitus completus* in another way. I teach an embrace in which, in its perfect realization, there is a complete dissipation of congestion, complete discharge of nervous surplus, complete relief from tension, and a complete satisfaction—an embrace peculiarly suited to the weak because its action is to increase the function of their ductless glands and to make strongly sexed individuals out of those previously afraid of sex or feeling themselves sexual failures, and which can also completely satisfy the normally strong.

But where the technique of the orgasmal school is followed, this embrace can hardly be realized, especially by those of powerful surplus. For everything in their technique tends to create a local congestion, which must find relief in orgasm, or distress follows. A "mutual, reciprocal, simultaneous friction" must certainly produce this result. I teach an alternation of friction, one positive while the other is passive, or else mutual quiet, magnetation and sublimation being the object. With them the whole matter is sexual and tends downwards to a sexual conclusion. With me the sexual magnetism is generated simply as a current on which to carry the love message, or by which to create the love light, all to be sublimated upwards to a romantic, poetic, spiritual conclusion, satisfying sex incidentally. They would concentrate the energy on the genitals, and I would diffuse it from the genitals throughout the system, from the sexual to the affectional, from sex-desire to romance, tenderness, spiritual exaltation and love, affording, I contend, more complete satisfaction than an orgasm, especially to the refined.

And their method requires always the use of contraceptives, or else observance of times and seasons (all such safeguards being conceded by the best authorities unsafe and unreliable), while my method may be used at any time, with "nothing between," and all of Nature's romance of touch unrestrained, with the certainty that where no semen discharges no conception occurs.

One believes he has discovered what becomes of the semen in Karezza—that it leaks backward and comes out in the urine. But better authorities claim that leakage of semen only occurs in diseased conditions, and not at all from continence. I think where the sublimation and absorption are carried to the right degree there is no leakage, but I think it possible that it occurs where the excitement exceeds the sublimation.

I am willing to concede that where the intercourse is of such a nature as to cause a congestion that is not sublimated, or where sexual congestion occurs and sublimation and magnetation are not available, the orgasm may have a necessary place. Perhaps it must be admitted that everything has somewhere its use.

The idea that when once the usual amount of semen has been secreted, secretion largely or completely ceases, only enough being secreted usually to replace what is absorbed, and this even under frequent or habitual sexual excitement, is, I believe, probably correct, and agrees with my own understanding of the matter. But ever and anon, with the usual man, a surplus does accumulate, is not sublimated, and an orgasm occurs.

The question of whether the woman's orgasm is essential to the best conception seems to have a new sidelight thrown upon it by the discussion concerning birthmarks and prenatal influence.

If, as most modern physicians seem to agree, there is no truth in the old theory of prenatal influence; if the germplasm is something separate, of which the individual sex-partner is only a carrier, as a postman carries a letter, but with the message within which he has nothing to do, then it would appear that the woman's orgasm or non-orgasm has as little influence as any other prenatal factor. Just as it would not really matter, so far as the message in the letter was concerned, provided it was delivered, whether the postman was quiet and normal, or had an epileptic fit at the moment of delivery, so it would not matter what the woman, or the man either, did or did not do, provided the ovum and sperm-cell were safely gotten together. Their motives and emotional states, according to this theory, do not count. Which would explain how a woman could be impregnated by the semen from a syringe; or bear a normal child even if raped; or if in a drug-sleep.

Again it must not be forgotten that conception, scientifically speaking, is the penetration of the ovum by the sperm cell and their coalescing. This rarely, if ever, occurs at the moment when the carriers are having their orgasm, but sometime after, often hours or even days after, at the moment when the sperm cell reaches the waiting egg. How can the previous orgasm have any effect then to devitalize him?

The idea that a child begotten where the mother has an orgasm would be more passionate or robust than where the mother has none may have a core of truth. A robust woman would, all other things being equal, be more likely to have an orgasm than a more mental type. This robustness, or lack of it, would likely be an inheritable character transmittable to the child as a trait of the strain. In other words, the orgasm would be a symptom of the mother's robustness, which the child would be likely to inherit, but would be in no sense a cause of that robustness or its inheritance. If the sperm-cell could get to the ovum of that woman, no matter how quiet she might be, the result would be just the same as if she had the most intense orgasm—unless indeed the magnetic state of the parents could have an effect to vitalize or demagnetize the germs, which is also something the skeptical modem physician rejects. Also her orgasm, in many cases, would be a symptom of her being "in heat," ripe for impregnation. But no matter how ripe she might be, if she were slow, the man fast, she could easily be impregnated without her own orgasm, with exactly the same results to her child. Which accounts for the well-attested fact that many women have been impregnated by the mere spattering of semen within the lips of the vulva. Finally, as to whether she did or did not get the orgasm would depend upon how much she was excited, not upon her procreative power at the time—as it is certain that a sterile woman may have intense orgasms.

To get the sperm-cell of a healthy male to the ovum of a healthy female is the one important matter in conception, and how it is done, provided it is effectually done, seems of minor importance, perhaps of no importance at all.

To sum up: The orgasmal school is honest but mistaken. Its fault is that it is a doctrine of the strong, only for the strong. Just as a wealthy man may spend money recklessly for a while and still not be poor, so a man rich in thyroxin and adrenalin may spend recklessly in orgasms for a while and not seem any the worse. And the method taught by the orgasmal school is such that it creates a demand, by congestion, for the orgasm, which must then occur or bad results follow. But for a weak man to follow their advice is very dangerous and courts a nervous breakdown, while my method builds him up. That orgasms are weakening is easily proven. Just as the way to get real facts about alcohol is to consult life-insurance companies, so to get facts about the orgasm go to the stockbreeder. Business has no sentiment or prejudice. Every stockbreeder will tell you that to permit a bull or stallion to serve too many or too often is to devitalize him.

21810697R00107

Printed in Great Britain
by Amazon